Super Cheap Adelaide Travel Guide 2020

Our Mission 6

Redefining Super Cheap 12

Discover Adelaide 14

Planning your trip 17

Hack your Adelaide Accommodation 20

The best price performance location in Adelaide 26

Use our FREE 27

accommodation finder service 27

How to be a green tourist in Adelaide 29

Saving money on Adelaide Food 31

SNAPSHOT: How to enjoy a $1,000 trip to Adelaide for $200 33

Unique bargains I love in Adelaide 34

Exchange Rate 35

How to use this book 36

OUR SUPER CHEAP TIPS... 37

Getting around 37

Start with this free tour 38

Go to a Free museum 40

Do a wine tour on the cheap 41

Visit the University 42

Cycle to Waterfall Gully 43

Visit the Adelaide Oval 44

Explore 29 parks	45
Henley Beach	46
Explore Adelaide Central Market	47
Visit Glenelg Beach	48
Explore Hahndorf	49
The Murray River	50
Enjoy free workouts	51
Get Cheap cinema tickets	52
Cheap Tuesday at the fringe festival	52
Food and drinks hacks	53
Nightlife	54
Not super cheap but loved	55
Visit Port Hughes	56
Swim with sea lions	57
Visit Kangaroo Island	58
Walk the Heysen Trail	59
Explore the outback	60
Cheapest route from the USA	63
Cheapest route from Europe	64
Need to Know	65
Cheap Eats	66
Avoid these tourist traps or scams	68
Religion	68

FREQUENTLY ASKED QUESTIONS 69

Getting out cheaply 70

Print or screenshot for easy reference 72

RECAP: How to have a $1,000 trip to Adelaide on a $205 budget 73

Ultimate Cheat Sheet 75

Thank you for reading 81

Bonus Budget Travel Hacks 85

How to find the freedom to travel 87

HOW TO FIND CHEAP FLIGHTS 91

Frequent Flyer Memberships 95

Pack like a Pro 96

Checks to Avoid Fees 97

Relaxing at the airport 99

Money: How to make it, spend it and save it while travelling 101

How to earn money WHILE travelling 102

How to spend money 104

How to save money while travelling 107

Travel Apps That'll Make Budget Travel Easier 109

How NOT to be ripped off 110

Small tweaks on the road add up to big differences in your bank balance 113

Where and How to Make Friends 116

When unpleasantries come your way…   117

Your Car rental insurance is crazy expensive   120

The best Travel Gadgets   125

Hacks for Families   127

Safety   130

Hilarious Travel Stories   132

How I got hooked on budget travelling   135

A final word…   137

Our Writers   138

Copyright   139

Our Mission

Like Simon Sinek said, "People don't buy what you do; they buy why you do it". We believe strongly that travel can and is best enjoyed on a budget.

Taking a trip to Adelaide is not just an outer journey, it's an inner one. Budget travel brings us closer to locals, culture and authenticity; which in turn makes our inner journeys more peaceful.

Travelling is painted as an expensive hobby; Travel guides, Travel bloggers and influencers often show you overpriced accommodation, restaurants and big-ticket attractions because they make money from our 'we're on vacation' mentality which leads to reckless spending. Our mission is to teach you how to enjoy more for less and get the best value from every dollar you spend in Adelaide.

This guide focuses on the cheap or free in Adelaide, but there is little value in travelling to Adelaide and not experiencing all it has to offer. Where possible we've included cheap workarounds or listed the experience in the loved but costly section - if it is worth your time and money.

We work to dispel myths, save you tons of money, teach you the local tips and tricks and help you find experiences in Adelaide that will flash before your eyes when you come to take your last breath on this beautiful earth.

Who this book is for and why anyone can enjoy budget travel

I've been travelling full-time for 20 years. I don't have a job and I'm not in any debt, which prompts friends and family to ask 'How can you afford to travel?'. My response? 'My passion is finding travel bargains'. This doesn't mean I do any less or sleep in dirty hostels. Someone who spends A LOT on travel hasn't planned or wants to spend their money. I believe you can live the bougie life on a budget; that's what I've been doing for the past 20 years.

Together with thrifty locals I met along the way I have funnelled my passion for travel bargains into 300 travel guides. In this guide, we have formulated a system to pass on to you, so you too can juice everything from visiting Adelaide while spending the least possible money.

There is a big difference between being cheap and frugal. I like to spend money on beautiful experiences, but 20 years of travel has taught me I could have a 20 cent experience that will stir my soul more than a $100 one. Of course, there are times when the reverse is true, my point is, spending money on travel is the best investment you can make but it doesn't have to be at levels set by hotels and attractions with massive ad spends and influencers who are paid small fortunes to get you to buy into something that you could have for a fraction of the cost.

I love travelling because it forces me to be present-minded. I like to have the cold hard budget busting facts to hand (which is why we've included so many one page charts, which you can use as a quick reference), but otherwise, I want to shape my own experience - and I'm sure you do too.

We have designed these travel guides to give you a unique planning tool to experience an unforgettable trip without spending the ascribed tourist budget.

When it comes to FUN budget travel, it's all about what you know. You can have all the feels without most of the bills. A few days spent planning can save you thousands. Luckily, Super Cheap Insider Guides have done the planning for you, so you can distill the information in minutes not days, leaving you to focus on what matters: immersing yourself in the sights, sounds and smells of Adelaide, meeting awesome new people and most importantly, feeling relaxed and happy. My sincere hope is that our tips will bring you great joy at a fraction of the price you expected.

So, grab a cup of tea, put your feet up and relax; you're about to enter the world of enjoying Adelaide on the cheap. Oh and don't forget a biscuit. You need energy to plan a trip of a lifetime on a budget.

Super Cheap Adelaide is <u>not</u> for travellers with the following needs:

1. You require a book with detailed offline travel maps. Super Cheap Insider Guides are best used with Google Maps - download before you travel to make the most of your time and money.
2. You would like thousands of accommodation, food and attraction recommendations; by definition, cheapest is most often singular. We only include maximum value recommendations. We purposively leave out over-priced attractions when there is no workaround.
3. You would like detailed write-ups about hotels/Airbnbs/Restaurants. We are bargain hunters first and foremost. We dedicate our time to finding the best deals, not writing flowery language about their interiors. Plus things change. If I had a pound for every time I read a Lonely Planet description only to find the place totally different, I would be a rich man. Always look at online reviews for the latest up to date information.

If you want to save A LOT of money while comfortably enjoying an unforgettable trip to Adelaide, minus the marketing, hype, scams and tourist traps read on.

Congratulations, you're saving money and doing Good!

We donate 10% of all book profits to charity.

This year we are donating to Animal Shelters including one in Adelaide.

The number of abandoned and homeless pets in Australia is estimated to be around 2 million. I'm sure you've seen your fair share of abandoned dogs during your travels: its heart wrenching to see man's best friend starving and alone.

'My dog Gracie was abandoned on the highway in Slovakia. At just ten months old, they tied her to the railings and left her there. Animal Hope picked her up and took care of her and found her a home with us. She is now a healthy, happy girl and loves travelling with us, getting her nose into new smells and soliciting belly rubs from fellow travellers. What breaks my heart is her 'I haven't been abandoned dance'. She is always so happy that we haven't abandoned her when we collect her from outside a supermarket that she dances on her leash for several minutes. Watch her 'I haven't been abandoned dance' dance   . Money could never buy the happiness she has brought my family and me, but donations can help other abandoned animals like her to find loving homes.'

Katherine Huber, a contributor to Super Cheap Vienna.

Donations are made on the 4th January of each year on profits from the previous year. To nominate a charity to receive 10% of the proceeds of sales from our 2020 editions complete the form here: supercheapinsiderguides.com

Gracie

Redefining Super Cheap

The value you get out of Super Cheap Adelaide is not based on what you paid for it; its based on what you do with it. You can only do great things with it, if you believe saving money is worth your time. Charging things to your credit card and thinking 'oh I'll pay it off when I get back' is something you won't be tempted to do if you change your beliefs now. Think about what you associate with the word cheap, because you make your beliefs and your beliefs make you.

I grew up thinking you had to spend more than you could afford to have a good time travelling. Now I've visited 190 countries I know nothing is further from the truth. Before you embark upon reading our specific tips for Adelaide think about your associations with the word cheap.

Here are the dictionary definitions of cheap:

1. costing very little; relatively low in price; inexpensive:
a cheap dress.
2. costing little labor or trouble:
Words are cheap.
3. charging low prices:
a very cheap store.
4. **of little account; of small value; mean; shoddy:**
cheap conduct; cheap workmanship.
5. **embarrassed; sheepish:**
He felt cheap about his mistake.
6. **stingy; miserly:**
He's too cheap to buy his own brother a cup of coffee.

Three out of six definitions have extremely negative connotations. The 'super cheap' we're talking about in this book is not shoddy, embarrassed or stingy. Hey, you've already donated to charity just by buying this book - how is that stingy? We added the super to reinforce our message. Super's dictionary definition stands for 'a super quality'. Super Cheap stands for enjoying the best on the lowest budget. Question other peoples definitions of cheap so you're not blinded to possibilities, potential, and prosperity. Here are some new associations to consider forging:

Shoddy

Cheap stuff doesn't last is an adage marketing companies have drilled into consumers. However by asking vendors the right questions cheap doesn't mean something won't last, I had a $10 backpack last for 8 years and a $100 suitcase bust on the first journey. A   out of San Francisco University found that people who spent money on experiences rather than things were happier. Memories last forever, not things, even expensive things. And as we will show you during this guide you don't need to pay to create great memories.

Embarrassed

I have friends who routinely pay more to vendors because they think their money is putting food on this person's table. Paradoxically, Cuban doctors are driving taxi's because they earn more money; it's not always a good thing for the place you're visiting to pay more and can cause unwanted distortion in their culture - Airbnb pushing out renters is an obvious example. Think carefully about whether the extra money is helping people or incentivising greed.

Stingy

Cheap can be eco-friendly. Buying thrift clothes is cheap but you also help the Earth. Many travellers are often disillusioned by the reality of traveling experience since the places on our bucket-lists are overcrowded. Cheap can take you away from the crowds. You can find balance and harmony being cheap. Remember,"A journey is best measured in friends, rather than miles." – Tim Cahill. And making friends is free!

A recent survey by Credit Karma found 50% of Millennials and Gen Z get into debt travelling. **Please don't allow credit card debt to be an unwanted souvenir you take home.** As you will see from this book, there's so much you can enjoy in Adelaide for free and so many ways to save money! You just need to want to!

Discover Adelaide

Moana beach.

Adelaide is a sophisticated, cosmopolitan city that is all about the finer things in life, but that doesn't mean they come with a big price tag. Here you can enjoy fine wine, finer food, fine beaches and fine people for a snip - as they say in Aussie - the name given to Australian slang.

Adelaide is home to 1.3 million people. I met many Adelaidean's who were keen to tell me no convicts were sent here! Count how many people tell you this - I bet it surpasses 10.

Adelaide was named after the wife of British king William IV. it has a liberal history as the first state to decriminalise homosexuality and legalise abortion. Women stood as MP's here from 1894.

History

Home to many indigenous tribes for thousands of years before European settlement began in 1836, Adelaide has since welcomed migrants from all over the world and is characterised by a great diversity of cultural traditions, languages spoken and systems of belief. The state of South Australia boasts a stable economy and low unemployment rate, with a broad base of thriving industries, including agriculture, wine, information and communications technology, automotive production, defence, biosciences, health, tourism and the arts.

Festivals

The city hosts many festivals, including WOMADelaide, the Adelaide, Festival of Arts and the Adelaide Fringe Festival, and has an extensive range of world-class sporting and recreational facilities. Known as the 20-minute city, Adelaide is easy to get around thanks to its broad boulevards and public transport network. Its central location makes it an ideal gateway to explore South Australia's many tourist attractions, from world-renowned wineries and rugged coastlines to the Australian outback.

Cuisine

Adelaides love their food. Over 100 fine dining restaurants exist alongside pop-up restaurants and food trucks. Adelaide is the wine capital of Australia, with well known brands such as Jacobs Creek growing their grapes nearby. There is no other city in the country which offers you such easy access to the vineyards. The Barossa Valley and Adelaide Hills are a short distance away.

Adelaide People

Adelaide is the city which is not just known for its heart stealing climate and natural beauty, but also for the people who are cherish helping others all the time. This picturesque city is full of amicable people who will go out of their way to help you. You will see a lot of Indian people, many Sikh, as well as women wearing the hijab, and there is also a strong Italian community.

How to make friends with the locals

It's not a city known for its night-life or party scene, but you will not struggle to strike up a conversation in and around the green space where flocks of parrots are in the trees. You can get around happily and inexpensively on public transport where people can often be seen striking up a conversation. It's a relaxing city that moves at a pace that will not age you quickly or generally make you weary over time so take the same approach to making friends with the locals.

Adelaide can be a budget-buster, but take heart. The trick to keeping your trip affordable is to get off the tourist track and find the local deals. Use this guide to make sure Adelaide leaves a lasting impression on your heart and mind, not your bank balance.

Planning your trip

The best time to visit

The first step in saving money on your Adelaide trip is timing. Go June to August or March to May or September. Rainfall is rare and daytime temperatures sit in the 60s and 70s and prices are lowest.

Stay in Airbnb

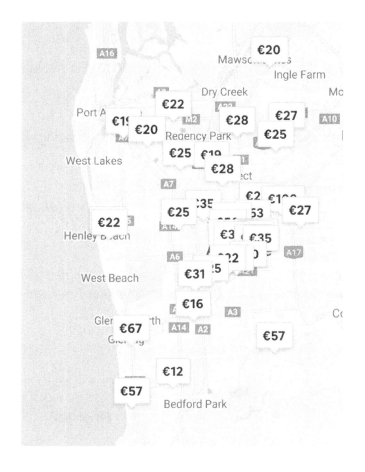

Airbnb's here are 70% cheaper than hotels. If you want to stay in hostels, we found Sunny's Adelaide Backpackers Hostel the best value. You can find a private room in the city for less than $20 or an entire apartment a bit further out for a similar price.

It is expensive to eat out so book an Airbnb and cook at home. You can buy great fresh produce from The Central market. No one wants to pay $30 for a mediocre salad - not even rich people.

Where to stay

Adelaide is an easy city to get around, so stay where you find the best Airbnb to suit your needs. Here are the main attractions:

North Terrace
Adelaide's cultural heart, with the SA Museum, Art Gallery of SA, State Library, Adelaide University and the Botanic Garden .

Rundle Mall
with over 800 stores to choose from, Rundle Mall is Adelaide's vibrant retail heart.

Central Market
the fresh produce heart of Adelaide, offering an amazing selection of fresh produce.

Rundle Street East
with a great selection of restaurants and bars only a few steps from a 99C bus stop.

Gouger Street
Adelaide's greatest selection of restaurants catering for all budgets and tastes and just a short walk from either free tram or bus stops

Top Cheap Sleeps under $30 - Airbnbs

1. https://www.airbnb.com/rooms/15185669?s=51
2. https://www.airbnb.com/rooms/10662281?s=51
3. https://www.airbnb.com/rooms/6059660?s=51
4. https://www.airbnb.com/rooms/19627210?s=51
5. https://www.airbnb.com/rooms/24765368?s=51

Hack your Adelaide Accommodation

Your two biggest expenses when travelling to Adelaide are accommodation and food. This section is intended to help you cut these costs dramatically before and while you are in Adelaide.

Hostels are the cheapest accommodation in Adelaide but there are some creative workarounds to upgrade your stay on the cheap.

Use Time

There are two ways to use time. One is to book in advance. Three months will net you the best deal, especially if your visit coincides with an event. The other is to book on the day of your stay. This is a risky move, but if executed well, you can lay your head in a five-star hotel for a 2-star fee.

Before I travelled to Adelaide, I checked for big events using a simple google search 'What's on in Adelaide', there were no big events drawing travellers so I risked showing up with no accommodation booked (If there are big events on demand exceeds supply and you should avoid using this strategy) I started checking for discount rooms at 11 am using a private browser on booking.com.

Before I go into demand-based pricing, take a moment to think about your risk tolerance. By risk, I am not talking about personal safety. No amount of financial savings is worth risking that. What I am talking about is being inconvenienced. Do you deal well with last-minute changes? Can you roll with the punches or do you dislike it if something changes? Everyone is different and knowing yourself is the best way to plan a great trip. If you are someone that likes to have everything pre-planned using demand-based pricing to get cheap accommodation will not work for you. Skip this section and go to blind-booking.

Demand-based pricing

Be they an Airbnb host or hotel manager; no one wants empty rooms. Most will do anything to make some revenue because they still have the same costs to cover whether the room is occupied or not. That's why you will find many hotels drastically slashing room rates for same-day bookings.

How to book five-star hotels for a two-star price

You will not be able to find these discounts when the demand exceeds the supply. So if you're visiting during the peak season, or during an event which has drawn many travellers don't try this.

On the day of your stay, visit booking.com (which offers better discounts than Kayak and agoda.com). Hotel Tonight individually checks for any last-minute bookings, but they take a big chunk of the action, so the better deals come from booking.com. The best results come from booking between 2 pm and 4 pm when the risk of losing any revenue with no occupancy is most pronounced, so algorithms supporting hotels slash prices. This is when you can find rates that are not within the "lowest publicly visible" rate. To avoid losing customers to other websites, or cheapening the image of their hotel most will only offer the super cheap rates during a two hour window from 2 pm to 4 pm. Two guests will pay 10x difference in price but it's absolutely vital to the hotel that neither knows it.

Takeaway: To get the lowest price book on the day of stay between 2 pm and 4 pm and extend your search radius to include further afield hotels with good transport connections.

How to trick travel Algorithms to get the lowest hotel price

Do not believe anyone who says changing your IP address to get cheaper hotels or flights does NOT work. If you don't believe us, download a Tor Network and search for flights and hotels to one destination using your current IP and then the tor network (a tor browser hides your IP address from algorithms. It is commonly used by hackers). You will receive different prices.

The price you see is a decision made by an algorithm that adjusts prices using data points such as past bookings, remaining capacity, average demand and the probability of selling the room or flight later at a higher price. If booking.com knows you've searched for the area before it will keep the prices high. To circumvent this, you can either use a different IP address from a cafe or airport or data from an international sim. I use a sim from Three, which provides free data in many countries around the world. When you search from a new IP address, most of the time, and particularly near booking you will get a lower price. Sometimes if your sim comes from a 'rich' country, say the UK or USA, you will see higher rates as the algorithm has learnt people from these countries pay more. The solution is to book from a local wifi connection - but a different one from the one you originally searched from.

How to get last-minute discounts on owner rented properties

In addition to Airbnb, you can also find owner rented rooms and apartments on www.vrbo.com or HomeAway or a host of others. Nearly all owners renting accommodation will happily give renters a "last-minute" discount to avoid the space sitting empty, not earning a dime.

Go to Airbnb or another platform and put in today's date. Once you've found something you like start the negotiating by asking for a 25% reduction. A sample message to an Airbnb host might read:

Dear HOST NAME,

I love your apartment. It looks perfect for me. Unfortunately, I'm on a very tight budget. I hope you won't be offended, but I wanted to ask if you would be amenable to offering me a 25% discount for tonight, tomorrow and the following day? I see that you aren't booked. I can assure you, I will leave your place exactly the way I found it. I will put bed linen in the washer and ensure everything is clean for the next guest. I would be delighted to bring you a bottle of wine to thank you for any discount that you could offer.

If this sounds okay, please send me a custom offer, and I will book straight away.

YOUR NAME.

In my experience, a polite, genuine message like this, that proposes reciprocity will be successful 80% of the time. Don't ask for more than 25% off, this person still has to pay the bills and will probably say no as your stay will cost them more in bills than they make. Plus starting higher, can offend the owner and do you want to stay somewhere, where you have offended the host?

In Practice

To use either of these methods, you must travel light. Less stuff means greater mobility, everything is faster and you don't have to check-in or store luggage. If you have a lot of luggage, you're going to have fewer of these opportunities to save on accommodation. Plus travelling light benefits the planet - you're buying, consuming, and transporting less stuff.

Blind-booking

If your risk tolerance does not allow for last-minute booking, you can use blind-booking. Many hotels not wanting to cheapen their brand with known low-prices, choose to operate a blind booking policy. This is where you book without knowing the name of the hotel you're going to stay in until you've made the payment. This is also sometimes used as a marketing strategy where the hotel is seeking to recover from past issues. I've stayed in plenty of blind book hotels. As long as you choose 4 or 5 star hotels, you will find them to be clean, comfortable and safe. priceline.com, Hot Rate® Hotels and Top Secret Hotels (operated by lastminute.com) offer the best deals.

Hotels.com Loyalty Program

This is currently the best hotel loyalty program with hotels in Adelaide. The basic premise is you collect 10 nights and get 1 free. hotels.com price match, so if booking.com has a cheaper price you can get hotel.com, to match. If you intend to travel more than ten nights in a year, its a great choice to get the 11th free.

Don't let time use you.

Rigidity will cost you money. You pay the price you're willing to pay, not the amount it requires a hotel to deliver. Therefore if you're in town for a big event, saving money on accommodation is nearly impossible so in such cases book three months ahead.

The best price performance location in Adelaide

A room near AdelaideX the local attractions, restaurants, and nightlife are within walking distance will save you time on transport. Restaurants and bars don't get that much cheaper the further you go from famous tourist attractions. But you will also get a better idea of the day to day life of a local if you stay in a neighbourhood like Elizabeth. It depends on the Adelaide you want to experience. For the tourist experience stay in the centre either in a last-minute hotel or Airbnb. For a taste of local life the leafy district of Elizabeth is the best you will find. Adelaide Riviera Hotel is a luxurious hotel with consistent last-minute rooms from $30 a night.

Use our FREE accommodation finder service

Feeling overwhelmed by all the accommodation options? Save yourself stress, hassle and time by using our FREE accommodation finder service.

We pride ourselves on actively helping our readers find the best price-performance accommodation. We normally charge $50 for this service, but for our paid readers it is FREE when you leave an honest review of this book. (Just a few short words like 'Excellent budget tips and insider insights' is all it takes).

So, how do you use the service?

Simply send our Services Manager, Amy Abraham the following information:

1.   A screenshot proof of purchase. (Go to your Amazon account, and click orders and make a screenshot of your purchase.)
2.   Send a screenshot of your review of the guide on Amazon.
3.   And answers to the following questions:

* What's your Budget? (e.g. lowest possible)
* How many are travelling and what are their ages?
* What Approximate location do you desire? (e.g. as close to the centre as possible/ near public transport)
* Do you have a strong dislike of either hostels or Airbnbs?

- If anyone in your group has mobility restrictions/ requires a lift/ no stairs etc?
- Add any details you think are pertinent to your needs.

About Amy and her team

Amy has travelled to over 170 countries personally and has recruited a team of bargain hunters to provide our accommodation finder service.

Send your details via E-mail to Amy Abraham at Amy@supercheapinsiderguides.com

What you'll receive

Amy and her team will work their magic. Within 24 hours you will be sent a list of the top three accommodations for your specific needs prioritised by which one we recommend.

We offer the same service for finding you the cheapest most direct flight. See our cheapest route to Adelaide for details.

If you would like to follow us on Facebook you can find us here: https://www.facebook.com/SuperCheapInsiderGuides/ . We also accept accommodation search requests via Facebook messenger, just make sure you send the necessary information listed above.

(Please note: If you received this book for free as part of a promotion, we cannot extend this service to you.)

How to be a green tourist in Adelaide

There is a bizarre misconception that you have to spend money to travel in an eco-friendly way. This like, all marketing myths was concocted and hyped by companies seeking to make money off of you. In my experience, anything with eco in front of their names e.g Eco-tours will be triple the cost of the regular tour. Don't get me wrong sometimes its best to take these tours if you're visiting endangered areas, but normally such places have extensive legislation that everyone, including the eco and non-eco tour companies, are complying with. The vast majority of ways you can travel eco-friendly are free and even save you money:

- Avoid Bottled Water - get a good water bottle and refill. The water in Adelaide is safe to drink.
- Thrift shop but check the labels and don't buy polyester clothes - overtime plastic is released into the ocean when we wash polyester.
- Don't put it in a plastic bag, bring a cotton tote with you when you venture out.
- Pack Light - this is one of the best ways to save money. If you find a 5-star hotel for tonight for $10, and you're at an Airbnb or hostel, you can easily pack and upgrade hassle-free. A light pack equals freedom and it means less to wash.
- Travel around Adelaide on Bikes or e-Scooters or use Public Transportation.
- Car Pool with services like bla bla car or Uber/Lyft share.
- Walk, this is the best way to get to know Adelaide. You never know what's around the corner.
- Travel Overland - this isn't always viable especially if you only have limited time off work, but where possible avoid flying and if you have to compensate by off-setting or

keeping the rest of your trip carbon-neutral by doing all of the above.

Saving money on Adelaide Food

Breakfast

If you stay somewhere with a free breakfast, eat smart. Don't eat sugary cereals or white flour rich pastries if you don't want to be hungry an hour later. Before leaving your hotel or checking out, find some fresh fruit, water, and granola in the fitness centre or coffee in the lobby or business centre. If your hotel doesn't have free breakfast, don't take it. You can always eat cheaper outside. Big Table has the best cheap breakfast we found.

Visit supermarkets at discount times.

You can get a 50 per cent discount around 5 pm at the Woolworths and Coles supermarkets on fresh produce. The cheaper the supermarket, the less discounts you will find, so check Woolworths and Coles and at 5 pm. Some items are also marked down due to sell-by date after the lunchtime rush so its also worth to check in around 3 pm.

Use delivery services on the cheap.

Take advantage of local offers on food delivery services. Most platforms including Menulog offer $10 off the first order in Adelaide.

Is the tap water drinkable?

Yes, refill around your water bottle at stations around the city.

How much can you save haggling here?

Not much, demand out strips supply. At the markets, you can potentially save 30%, elsewhere I didn't have 'much go' which is Aussie slang for it didn't work out.

SNAPSHOT: How to enjoy a $1,000 trip to Adelaide for $200

(full breakdown at the end of the guide)

Stay	private room close to the city - https://www.airbnb.com/rooms/21152790?s=51 $13 https://www.airbnb.com/rooms/17451897?s=51 this one is also a good option in the city. Or use this accommodation finder service.
Eat	Average meal cost: $10
Move	Use free bikes/ buses. Long distance greyhound bus cost: $40
See	Botanical gardens. Beaches, churches, free live music. Tour a vineyard $70
Total	US$200

Unique bargains I love in Adelaide

Beautiful beaches, historical towns, peculiar villages on hill-tops, and abundant wildlife make Adelaide a stunning land-scape to explore for free. There's Free bikes, bottomless coffees from Hungry Jacks, bakeries, Blessed Cheese Deli and Oxfam books are my favourite Adelaide bargains. I loved cycling everywhere, the city is flat, and you can take the bike trains for free.

Exchange Rate

Amount

1

From

USD
US Dollar

AUD
Australian Dollar

To

1 USD =

1.39471 AUD

1 AUD = 0.716997 USD
1 USD = 1.39471 AUD

US Dollar to Australian Dollar Conversion

Last updated: 2019-01-20 12:5

How to use this book

Google and Tripadvisor are your on-the-go guides while travelling, a travel guide adds the most value during the planning phase, and if you're without wifi. Always download the google map for your destination - having an offline map will make using this guide much more comfortable. For ease of use, we've set the book out the way you travel starting with arriving, how to get around, then on to the money-saving tips. The tips we prioritised according to when you need to know the tip to save money, so free tours and combination tickets feature first. We prioritised the rest of the tips by how much money you can save and then by how likely it was that you would be able to find the tip with a google search. Meaning those we think you could find alone are nearer the bottom.. I hope you find this layout useful. If you have any ideas about making Super Cheap Insider Guides easy to use, please email me philgattang@gmail.com .Now let's get started with juicing the most pleasure from your trip to Adelaide with the least possible money.

OUR SUPER CHEAP TIPS...

Getting around

Rent a free bike!

Like a growing number of cities around the world, Adelaide has a bike-sharing program, and it's free! Adelaide is a lovely city to cycle with routes out to most of the beaches and attractions. Learn more about how to take advantage of the free bikes here: https://www.bikesa.asn.au/adelaide-freebikes

Start with this free tour

Forget exploring the city by wandering around aimlessly. Start with a free organised tour. Nothing compares to local

advice, especially when travelling on a budget. Ask for their recommendations for the best cheap eats, the best bargains, the best markets, the best place for a particular street eat. Perhaps some of it will be repeated from this guide, but it can't hurt to ask, especially if you have specific needs or questions. At the end you should leave an appropriate tip (usually around $5), but nobody bats an eye lid if you are unable or unwilling to do so, tell them you will leave a good review and always give them a little gift from home - I always carry small Vienna fridge magnets and I always tip the $5, but it is totally up to you.

This is the free tour I did. I thought it was a great introduction to the city and covered the main attractions. You can book here: http://www.adelaidefreewalkingtour.com.au/

Go to a Free museum

Go to South Australian Museum. It has the largest exhibition of Aboriginal Art and History. And it is FREE!

Afterwards Enjoy a free chocolate tour at nearby Haigh chocolate factory. You can book a free tour online. https://www.haighschocolates.com.au/tours

Do a wine tour on the cheap

Adelaide is one of the ten wine capitals of the world. Barossa Valley, the Adelaide Hills or McLaren Vale are just one hour from the city (opposite directions of the city though). Each wine valley is absolutely beautiful, and offers amazing wine. There's also some breweries and distilleries throughout the regions. You need to go as part of a tour for access - https://www.viator.com/tours/Barossa-Valley/Barossa-Valley-Day-Trip-from-Adelaide-including-Aussie-Barbecue-Lunch/d5623-24545P1 is the one I did, $70 for a full-day.

Visit the University

The building is stunning. Use your free city bike to get there
https://www.bikesa.asn.au/adelaidefreebikes. Adelaide University boasts four Nobel Peace Prize winners including Sir Howard Walter Florey for the discovery of penicillin. Enjoy the University's stunning grounds.

Cycle to Waterfall Gully

Just put the name into google maps and cycle there. It is a breathtakingly beautiful walk and waterfall.

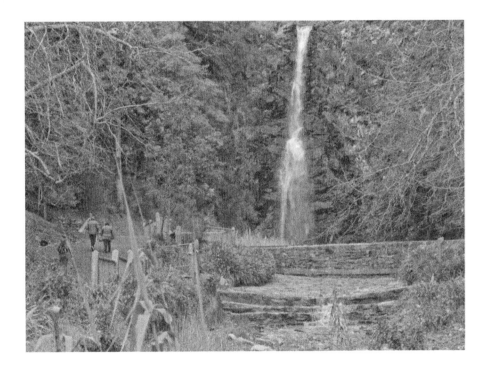

Visit the Adelaide Oval

Check out some games of AFL or cricket, or just wander by and hear the crowd roar on Friday nights. Cheap tickets can be found here https://www.raa.com.au

Explore 29 parks

Locals are kind and friendly and the parks are great meeting places. The **Botanical Park is my favourite. Here is a full list of all 29:** https://adelaideparklands.com.au/parks-and-squares/

Henley Beach

Go at Sunset for spectacular views - cycle or take bus H30, from Stop T2 or U2 Southside every half hour and takes 35 minutes.

⏻ INSIDER INSIGHT

An hour's drive from Adelaide is another worldly place called Fleurieu Peninsula. It was named after French man Nicolas Baudin in 1802 after he explored south coast of Australia. You can find over 30 different whale species here as well as beaches surfing, scuba and snorkelling, sailing and swimming.

Explore Adelaide Central Market

Watch cheese being made and feast on chocolate samples at this 143 year old market.

Afterwards Hit up Oxfam Books on Hutt Street for some cheap awesome reads for those long Greyhound rides or to find a $1 book to sell for $500!

Visit Glenelg Beach

It is a beautiful beach town with a Main Street to walk with shops and good eateries. You can cycle there with a free bike or take the red line tram. End destination GLNELG.

Explore Hahndorf

About 45 minutes up the freeway is a beautiful little German town that I absolutely love. Hahndorf has great shops and atmosphere. Go in fall for the most amazing colours.

The Murray River

Third longest river in the world runs through Adelaide.

Take a picnic to Rymill Park and sit by the Murray River or go to Murray Bridge.

💡 INSIDER INSIGHT

Wild dolphins live in Port River. They are Indo-Pacific bottlenose dolphins. They are wild and free but have chosen to call the Port River heir home. The cheapest way to get up close and personal is on the Dolphin Explore Boat: https://www.dolphinexplorer.com.au/bookings/

Enjoy free workouts

The Goodlife Adelaide City gym offers a FREE 5 Day Pass . https://www.goodlifehealthclubs.com.au/clubs/adelaide-city/. Don't mention anything about travelling through. They are offering you the pass for free to convert you into a paying member. Don't feel bad, think of all the money you've paid gyms and never used their services. You can also leave them a review online if you feel bad for using their facilities for free.

Free yoga

Sign-up for free yoga classes: https://www.meetup.com/topics/free-yoga-classes/au/adelaide/

Get Cheap cinema tickets

Mercury Cinema: This cinema is a little different to most. Being a cinema club, it doesn't offer single tickets; you need to buy a membership (for four films, ten films or a year of films). But these are very good value, as you end up paying between $2.50 to $10.00 per screening. The cinema shows new release films alongside a retrospective program, however its new releases are generally ones from film festivals or those that aren't getting screened elsewhere.

Cheap Tuesday at the fringe festival

If you're heading to Adelaide Fringe, check out Cheap Tuesday for up to 70% off tickets.

Food and drinks hacks

Bottomless coffee at Hungry Jacks

Go to any Hungry Jacks around the city for unlimited coffee refills and free wifi.

Best Bang for your buck all-you-can-eat

Fresh Choice Restaurant has an all-you-can-eat buffet during the week. Good quality fresh food for $20.
Address: 373 Diagonal Rd.

Food trucks

Veggie Velo was the best food truck I ate at in Adelaide.

Nightlife

Head to Rundle Street, the city's hub for events, street parades and parties. Happy hours start at 5pm. The Elephant British Pub is the best happy hour I found, most drinks including cocktails $5.

Rooftop bars

If you love rooftop bars go to 2KW, The Majestic Hotel or Florence Rooftop Bar. If you're not overly concerned about the view just check out the laneways (off Rundle St or Hindley St) to find cute little bars and great restaurants, there are dozens.

Free comedy

The Rhino room offers a double free pass if you enter your details to become an Adelaide Comedy Member. http://www.rhino-room.com.au/

Not super cheap but loved

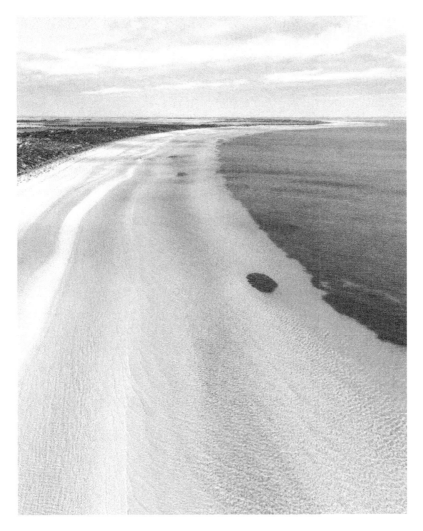

Port Hughes

Visit Port Hughes

Just west of Adelaide, in South Australia's Yorke Peninsula is stunning Port Huges. You can take a bus from the central train station to Moonta Cnr Henry & Milne and a taxi from there. Round-trip is $60.

Swim with sea lions

You can do this for free at Port Lincoln. You can take a cheap flight there with Jetstar circa $65 single.

Visit Kangaroo Island

SeaLink operates the ferry service to Kangaroo Island. Each crossing takes **approximately 45 minutes** and departs from Cape Jervis which is a 1.5 hour drive south of Adelaide. It costs 27.50 return. https://www.sealink.com.au/ the island is definitely worth the trip but pack snacks. Sealink also operate the bus from Adelaide Central Bus Station to Cape Jervis which costs $17 each way. DO NOT BUY A COMBO TICKET - it works out cheaper as singles and they time the ferries for the bus arrivals.

Walk the Heysen Trail

This impressive 1,200km walking route. Bus Premier State-liner is going there for $60 return.

Explore the outback

Go north up to the Flinders Ranges to experience some of the outback. It's a 6 hour drive. I saw prices as low as $60 for the day as a group of 10. Hostels are the best place to book it.

Websites to save you Money

1. **TalkTalkbnb.com** - Here you stay for free when you teach the host your native language
2. Rome2Rio.com - the go to site for good travel prices on train, bus, planes etc. Especially good for paths less travelled.
3. couchsurfing.com - stay for free with a local - always check reviews.
4. trustedhousesitter.com - always check reviews
5. booking.com - now sends you vouchers for discounts in the city when you book through them
6. airbnb.com for both accommodation and experiences.
7. hostelbookers.com - book hostels
8. https://www.groupon.com.au/coupons/adelaide - daily deals.
9. http://www.adelaidefreewalkingtour.com.au/ - free walking tour.

Shows or Films made in, or about Adelaide

'Return Home' 1990

It's set in a fictionalised western Adelaide suburb, and shot mostly around Henley Beach and other parts of West/South Adelaide. It's about a bloke who grew up in the area coming back after moving interstate for his career. Because of this film I always associate the second movement from Dvořák's Ninth Symphony with that area.

Cheapest route from the USA

At the time of writing Jetstar are flying to Adelaide return from $560 out of Honolulu. I specialise in finding cheap flights, so if you need help finding a cheap flight simply review this book and send me an email. philgtang@gmail.com

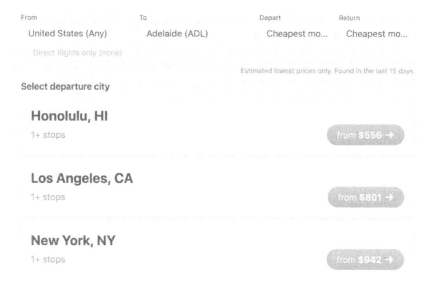

From	To	Depart	Return
United States (Any)	Adelaide (ADL)	Cheapest mo...	Cheapest mo...

Direct flights only (none)

Estimated lowest prices only. Found in the last 15 days.

Select departure city

Honolulu, HI
1+ stops

from $556 →

Los Angeles, CA
1+ stops

from $801 →

New York, NY
1+ stops

from $942 →

Cheapest route from Europe

At the time of writing Qantas are flying to Adelaide from London for $690 return. I specialise in finding cheap flights, so if you need help finding a cheap flight simply review this book and send me an email. philgtang@gmail.com

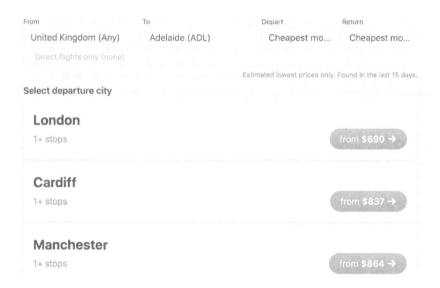

From	To	Depart	Return
United Kingdom (Any)	Adelaide (ADL)	Cheapest mo...	Cheapest mo...
Direct flights only (none)			

Estimated lowest prices only. Found in the last 15 days.

Select departure city

London
1+ stops — from $690 →

Cardiff
1+ stops — from $837 →

Manchester
1+ stops — from $864 →

(Please send me a screenshot of your review - with your flight hacking request). I aim to reply to you within 12 hours. If it's an urgent request mark the email URGENT in the subject line and I will endeavour to reply ASAP.

If you're travelling from outside Europe or the USA, I can also help you find the lowest cost direct flight. Simply review this book and email me.

Need to Know

Currency: Australian Dollar

Language: English / Aussie Slang

Money: Widely available ATMs.

Visas: http://www.doyouneedvisa.com/

Mobile Data:

Many telecoms providers will allow you to roam free in Australia. Check your plan, if not pick up a Telstra prepaid SIM.

Time: GMT + 9.5

When to Go

High Season: March to May

Shoulder: September to November

Low Season: December to March.

Important Numbers

000 Ambulance

000 Police

Watch to understand the History

Adelaide's history is fascinating. There are tons of documentaries. This is a 5 minute one that gives you a good overview - https://www.youtube.com/watch?v=gTaUIShldFl

Cheap Eats

Fill your stomach without emptying your wallet by trying these local restaurants with mains under $10.

(Download the offline map on google maps, (instructions 1. go to app 2. select offline apps in the left sidebar 3. go to the area you want to download 4. click download). Then simply type the restaurant names in to navigate, star them so you can see where the cheap eats are when you're out and about to avoid wasting your money at hyped tourist joints)

The Flying Fig Deli
bagels (starting at AUD$6.50) and eggs on organic sourdough rye with beetroot remoulade (AUD$9.90).
Address: 161 Jeffcott Street

Burger Theory
burger (AUD$10) comes with lettuce, tomato and American cheese in a brioche bun. The Number 2 (AUD$12) features a blue cheese sauce, onion confit and bacon.
Address: 8-10 Union Street,

Sit Lo
Delve into a cone of crispy lotus root chips (AUD$4.50).
Address: 30 Bank Street

Lucia's
Poached eggs, tomatoes and mushrooms on artisan bread (AUD$13.50) will fill you up; the spaghetti carbonara (AUD$13.50), and the spaghetti vongole (AUD$15) are also particularly good.
Address: Stall 1, Adelaide Central Market, Grote Street.

Kutchi Deli Parwana

Wrap your lips around fried dumplings stuffed with leek and topped with lamb mince and split pea sauce (AUD$13). Nibble on chicken pieces marinated in yoghurt and Afghan spices (AUD$15). 7 Ebenezer Place, Adelaide city centre

Chinatown Café
Great cheap Chinese food.
Address: 38-41 Moonta Street, Chinatown

Star of Siam
Great Thai.
Address: 67 Gouger Street

Bodri's Hungarian Artisan Bakery & Cafe

Awesome, cheap baked goods.
My favourite food trucks were Moorish Bites Food Truck, Moroccan, Mum and Meloui Manufacture a Great Moment and Veggie Velo Food Truck - Good wholesome and delicious veggie burgers.

Avoid these tourist traps or scams

I didn't hear of any scams in Adelaide only that I shouldn't use the local taxis. Use Uber in Adelaide, it is common here for traditional taxi's to overcharge.

Religion

Religion in Adelaide is secular mainly. 44.7% said they had no religion. The largest single religion in the City of Adelaide was (Roman) Catholic. There are definitely more pubs than churches.

FREQUENTLY ASKED QUESTIONS

1. Is it safe to travel Adelaide alone?

Absolutely.

2. What's the weather like in Adelaide?

Adelaide has a welcoming climate made up of pleasant, warm summers and mild, short winters. In the hotter months, expats will find themselves with over 14 hours of sunlight, but with plenty of opportunity to find respite in the form of a beach. Most of the rain in Adelaide falls between April and October.

3. How long does it take to get to Melbourne?

It is a 9 hour bus.

Getting out cheaply

At the time of writing Jetstar are offering the cheapest flights onwards. Take advantage of discounts and specials. Sign up for e-newsletters from local carriers including Jetstar to learn about special fares. Be careful with cheap airlines, most will allow **hand-luggage only**, and some charge for anything that is not a backpack. Check their websites before booking if you need to take luggage.

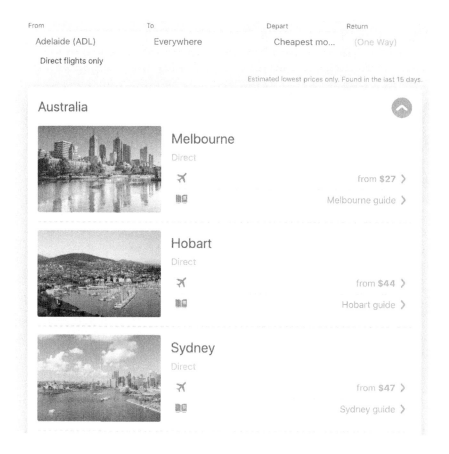

From	To	Depart	Return
Adelaide (ADL)	Everywhere	Cheapest mo...	(One Way)
Direct flights only			

Estimated lowest prices only. Found in the last 15 days.

Australia

Melbourne
Direct

✈ from $27 ›

📖 Melbourne guide ›

Hobart
Direct

✈ from $44 ›

📖 Hobart guide ›

Sydney
Direct

✈ from $47 ›

📖 Sydney guide ›

Cheapest Bus Out

Firefly Express is the cheapest bus provider for onward destinations from Adelaide. http://www.fireflyexpress.com.au/ Melbourne is $35 and Alice Springs is $110. It is much better and cheaper to fly to other destinations due to the vast distances you will have to cover.

Print or screenshot for easy reference

	How	Cost normally	Cost when following suggested tip
Stay	airbnb in the city - https://www.airbnb.com/rooms/21727317?s=51 $10	Hotels are upwards of $150 a night.	$10/ night x 5
Tastiest street foods to try	Veggie Velo food truck.	$250 eating out. You don't have to spend a lot to enjoy incredible food in Adelaide.	$6 - $10 - two meals out a day. Total cost $60
Get around	free bike	$50 in Ubers	$0
See	Beaches, wine valley trips	$300	$70 half day tour of the vineyards
Get out	Jetstar to Melbourne $25	$75	$25
Total		$1425 saving $1,220	$205

RECAP: How to have a $1,000 trip to Adelaide on a $205 budget

Five star hotels
Last minute 5 star hotels deals. Check on the same day of your stay for cheap five star hotel deals. Go to booking.com enter Adelaide, tonight, only one night and filter by 5 stars. In business cities this can be very effective in the low season on the weekends when hotels empty of their business travellers. Potential saving $800.

Restaurant deals
Nearly every restaurant in Adelaide offers a midday menu for lunch at around $7. If you're on a budget, but like eating out, consider doing your dining in the daytime.
Potential saving $100.

Go to museums/ attractions for free
The average traveller spends $80 on attractions in Adelaide. The free museum and tours are equally as great - and free! Potential saving $80.

Drink outdoors with friends
Adelaide is super green and the best way to experience the city is to buy a couple of beers from a supermarket and enjoy them somewhere green, or near the beach. A beer costs around $8 in a bar. Potential savings on drinks $50 assuming you have three beers a day - hey you're on vacation!

Book ahead

Book buses six weeks in advance for the cheapest prices.
Potential savings: $150

Ultimate Cheat Sheet

Get from the airport	Jetexpress - https://www.adelaidemetro.com.au/Timetables-Maps/Special-Services/Airport-services - Metro offers an express double decker bus service called JetExpress between the airport and the city the J1 service, it costs around 6 dollars.
Get Around	free bike or bus/tram
Stay	airbnb, much cheaper than even hostels
Eat	Bagels at The Flying Fig Deli
Do	Mount Lofty
Sunset	Marina Sunset Bar
Best Budget Experiences	Explore a historic ship $13 - https://abnb.me/o204vGbSfT?s=51
Cheapest Onward Destination	Melbourne by plane Greyhound covers many routes but are expensive. From Melbourne you can buy a hop on and hof off pass - https://www.greyhound.com.au/coach-travel/travel-passes/travel-passes-products?category=hop-on-hop-off&homepage_passes_3

The secret to saving HUGE amounts of money when travelling to Adelaide is...

Your mindset. Money is an emotional topic, if you associate words like cheapskate, Miser (and its £9.50 to go into Charles Dickens London house, oh the Irony) with being thrifty when travelling you are likely to say 'F-it' and spend your money needlessly because you associate pain with saving money. You pay now for an immediate reward. Our brains are prehistoric; they focus on surviving day to day. Travel companies and hotels know this and put trillions into making you believe you will be happier when you spend on their products or services. Our poor brains are up against outdated programming and an onslaught of advertisements bombarding us with the message: spending money on travel equals PLEASURE. To correct this carefully lodged propaganda in your frontal cortex you need to imagine your future self.

Saving money does not make you a cheapskate. It makes you smart. How do people get rich? They invest their money. They don't go out and earn it; they let their money earn more money. So every time you want to spend money, imagine this: while you travel your money is working for you, not you for money. While you sleep the money you've invested is going up and up. That's a pleasure a pricey entrance fee can't give you. Thinking about putting your money to work for you tricks your brain into believing you are not withholding pleasure from yourself, you are saving your money to invest so you can go to even more amazing places. You are thus turning thrifty travel into a pleasure fueled sport.

When you've got money invested - If you want to splash your cash on a first-class airplane seat - you can. I can't tell you how to invest your money, only that you should. Saving $20 on taxi's doesn't seem like much but over time you could be saving upwards of $15,000 a year, which is a deposit for a house which you can rent on Airbnb to finance more travel. Your brain making money looks like your brain on cocaine, so tell yourself saving money is making money.

Scientists have proved that imagining your future self is the easiest way to associate pleasure with saving money. You can download FaceApp — which will give you a picture of what you will look like older and greyer, or you can take a deep breath just before spending money and ask yourself if you will regret the purchase later.

The easiest ways to waste money travelling are:

Getting a taxi. The solution to this is to always download the google map before you go. Many taxi drivers will drive you around for 15 minutes when the place you were trying to get to is a 5-minute walk... remember while not getting an overpriced taxi to tell yourself, 'I am saving money to free myself for more travel.'

Spending money on overpriced food when hungry. The solution: carry snacks. A banana and an apple will cost you, in most places less than a dollar.

Spending on entrance fees to top-rated attractions. If you really want to do it, spend the money happily. If you're conflicted sleep on it. I don't regret spending $200 on a skydive over the Great Barrier Reef, I do regret going to the top of the shard in London for $60. Only you can know but make sure it's your decision and not the marketing directors at said top-rated attraction.

Telling yourself 'you only have the chance to see/eat/experience it now'. While this might be true, make sure YOU WANT to spend the money. Money spent is money you can't invest, and often you can have the same experience for much less.

You can experience luxurious travel on a small budget which will trick your brain into thinking you're already a high-roller, which will mean you'll be more likely to start acting like one and invest your money. Stay in five-star hotels for $5 by booking on the day of your stay on booking.com to enjoy last minute deals. You can go to fancy restaurants using daily deal sites. Ask your airline about last minute upgrades to first-class or business. I paid $100 extra on a $179 ticket to Cuba from Germany to be bumped to Business Class. When you ask you will be surprised what you can get both at hotels and airlines.

Travel, as the saying goes is the only thing you spend money on that makes you richer. In practice, you can easily waste money, making it difficult to enjoy that metaphysical wealth. The biggest money saving secret is to turn bargain hunting into a pleasurable activity, not an annoyance. Budgeting consciously can be fun, don't feel disappointed because you don't spend the $60 to go into an attraction, feel good because soon that $60 will soon be earning money for you. Meaning you'll have the time and money to enjoy more metaphysical wealth, while your bank balance increases.

PRACTICAL THINGS TO REMEMBER TO SAVE MONEY

- Download google maps for for use offline.
- Bring a good mosquito spray or combine a few drops of lemongrass oil with a moisturiser. Mosquitos are a nuance in summertime.
- Know the names of foods to try and the star the restaurants to try them at on Google Maps.
- Don't eat at any restaurants with touts outside.
- Go away from the main thoroughfare in Adelaide for cheaper restaurant prices
- Pack food for the airport, you'll save $10 on a bad cup of coffee and stale croissant at the airport.

So there it is, you can save a small fortune by being strategic with your trip planning. We've arranged everything in the guide to offer the best bang for your buck. Which means we took the view that if it's not a good investment for your money, we wouldn't include it. Why would a guide called 'Super Cheap' include lots of overpriced attractions? That said if you think we've missed something or have unanswered questions ping me an email philgtang@gmail.com I'm on central Europe time and usually reply within 8 hours of getting your mail.

Don't put your dreams off!

Time is a currency you never get back and travel is its greatest return on investment. Plus now you know you can visit Adelaide for a fraction of the price most would have you believe.

Henley Pier

Thank you for reading

Dear Lovely Reader,

If you have found this book useful, please consider writing a short review on Amazon.

One person from every 1000 readers leaves a review on Amazon. It would mean more than you could ever know if you were one of our 1 in 1000 people to take the time to write a short review.

We are a group of four friends who all met travelling 15 years ago. We believe that great experiences don't need to blow your budget, just your mind.

Thank you so much for reading again and for spending your time and investing your trips future in Super Cheap Insider Guides.

One last note, please don't listen to anyone who says 'Oh no, you can't visit Adelaide on a budget'. Unlike you they didn't have this book. The truth is you can do ANYWHERE on a budget with the right insider advice and planning. Sure, learning to travel to Adelaide on a budget that doesn't compromise on anything or drastically compromise on safety or comfort levels is a skill, but this guide has done the detective work for you. Now it is time for you to put the advice into action.

Phil

P.S If you need any more super cheap tips we'd love to hear from you e-mail me at philgtang@gmail.com, we have a lot of contacts in every region, so if there's a specific bargain you're hunting we can help you find it :-)

Are you visiting Melbourne next? Save more money on your adventure with Super Cheap Melbourne.

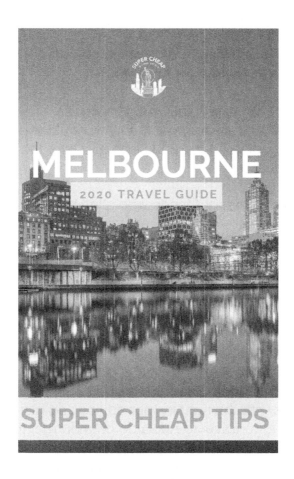

SHOP 150 VACATIONS UNDER $150.

INCLUDING LONDON.

SUPERCHEAPINSIDERGUIDES.COM

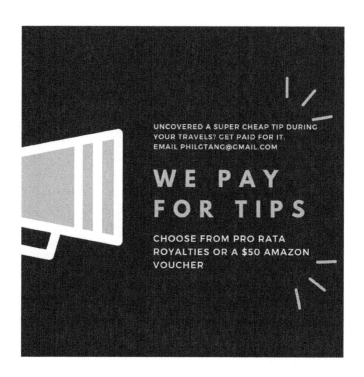

UNCOVERED A SUPER CHEAP TIP DURING
YOUR TRAVELS? GET PAID FOR IT.
EMAIL PHILGTANG@GMAIL.COM

WE PAY
FOR TIPS

CHOOSE FROM PRO RATA
ROYALTIES OR A $50 AMAZON
VOUCHER

Bonus Budget Travel Hacks

I've included these bonus travel hacks to help you plan and enjoy your trip to Adelaide cheaply, joyfully and smoothly. Perhaps they will even inspire you or renew your passion for long-term travel.

From saving space in your pack to scoring cheap flights, there are a wealth of generic travel hacks to help you enjoy stress-free, happier travels without breaking the bank. This is why I've included this bonus section to maximise the value you get from buying this book.

When I tell people I write a travel guide series focused on luxurious budget travel, they wrongly assume that's impossible and often say 'Hitchhiking and couch-surfing?'. Others with more vivid imaginations ask me if I recommend hooking up with older men or women… Of course, they are surprised when I tell them that not one of the 150 Super Cheap Guides endorses such practises because they maximise discomfort. They look at me dumbfounded and ask 'How on earth do you travel comfortably on a budget then?'

Travelling cheaply in a way that doesn't compromise enjoyment, comfort or safety is a skill I have honed over 20 years of travelling. My foremost learning was that locals always know the tricks and tips to enjoy the same or a better tourist experience for a 10th of the cost, and that's why I teamed up with locals in each locale to distil the tips that will save you a fortune without compromising on enjoyment or comfort.

Enjoyable budget travel is about balancing and prioritising what is important to you.
When I tell people about my methodology I often receive long defensive monologues about why they spend so much on travel, or why they can't or don't travel. Thats why we will first discuss how you can find the freedom to travel.

How to find the freedom to travel

Freedom is one of those words that can mean different things to different people. It's important to be clear on what it looks like to you in your life, and all the stories and beliefs that prevent you from having it. For me, freedom means always having at choice in my life. I don't do anything that I don't want to do. —LEO BABAUTA

We've spoken a lot about how to save money travelling to Adelaide, but how do you find the freedom if you have:

1. Pets
2. Kids
3. A spouse who doesn't want you to travel
4. A job that keeps you at home?

Like everything, there's a solution to every problem. In this chapter, I want to you to think about whether your excuses can be overcome using the following solutions, because as Randy Komisar said: "And then there is the most dangerous risk of all – the risk of spending your life not doing what you want on the bet you can buy yourself the freedom to do it later."

Pets

I have a dog, an extremely loving German Shepherd. And when I travel overland from Austria she comes with me and my wife. If we are heading on a longer trip we either leave her with friends or family or we get someone to house sit for us. housesitters.com offers up people who are vetted and reviewed and in exchange for free accommodation will care for your pets. Just be aware it often works out financially better to rent your space on Airbnb and pay someone to look after your pets. Make sure you visit their facilities before you entrust your pet to anyone and of course, always read the reviews.

I know a lot of people miss their pets travelling which is why we endeavour to take our dog with us. Exploring with her has formed some of our most precious memories. If you're flying with your pet always look up the rules and make sure you comply. If you're going to the UK for example, they quarantine dogs who come in by air. So we only take our dog by car. Coming into the UK by car, dogs must need to be chipped, have a note from a vet saying they are clear of Rabies and tapeworms, have a pet passport and be on a course of medication for tapeworms 2 days before they enter. The UK is the strictest country I've encountered when it comes to travelling with pets so I use this as barometer. My point is, do your homework if you're bringing your furry friend, both about entry conditions and the local environment for your pet. For instance, in India, many domesticated dogs are attacked by street dogs. Educate yourself on your options and limitations but don't think because you have pets that travel is out of the question.

Kids

I also have a daughter who is about to turn 1. We have travelled to seven countries with her so far, with many more in the pipeline. The easiest way to travel with kids is in an RV. You don't have to worry about checking vast amounts of baggage or travelling with a stroller. You have unlimited freedom and can camp for free in many places. You can normally take the RV on a slow ship cheaper than the price of a plane ticket for 3 people.

A study by Cornell University found that we get more happiness from anticipating a travel experience in comparison to anticipating buying a new possession, so in that way, money can buy you happiness. If you invest in an RV, you can also turn it into a profit centre by renting it out on platforms like www.outdoorsy.com.

You don't necessarily have to fly to travel with kids, train, bus and RV's are better options. Kids become more adaptable and flexible when the world is their classroom. This is true at any age. but when kids immerse themselves in new places and engage with local cultures; this open-mindedness helps them in all aspects of their lives. For school-age children, you are limited to holiday dates, but with 12 weeks off a year, you can still find adventure together.

A spouse who doesn't want you to travel

A loving partner should always want what's best for you. Scientifically, travelling is proven to reduce stress. A study in 2000 study found that men and women who do not take a trip for several years are 30 per cent more likely to have a heart attack. It makes sense because when you travel you are more active; travellers often walk ten miles a day, sightseeing and soaking up new sights and smells.

Travelling also strengthens the 'openness' aspect of your personality and makes you less emotionally reactive to day-to-day changes, improving emotional stability. Sure, losing your baggage or almost missing a connecting flight can be panic-inducing, but, overall, the data supports that travelling is beneficial for you. Tell your partner about these studies, if they don't want a healthier, happier, more emotionally stable you, then it may be time to consider why you're investing your time with this person.

Another common issue is mismatched travel budgets. If you and your partner travel together and they force you to overspend with the 'we're on holiday/vacation!' appendage, here's a tip from one of our writers Kim:

'My husband and I were always having 'discussions' about money during our trips. I love bargains and he is the kind of traveller who's totally cool to be ripped off because he normally travels for business and has become used to spending corporate money. The compromise we reached is that he reads a shoestring or super cheap guide before the trip. Then when he wants to waste money, I say yes, but only in exchange for doing one budget item from the guide. It has worked wonders, lessened our 'discussions' and he now actually chooses cheaper destinations as he sees budgeting as a game.'

A job that keeps you at home

Our lives can feel constantly busy. Sometimes we may feel we are sinking beneath our workload. If you're close to or suffering a burnout the stress relief that comes from novelty and change in the form of new people, sights and experiences is the best remedy you could give to yourself.

If you're in a job that is hurting your health or well-being its time to reconsider why. It is often the case that you believe the work to be deeply rewarding, but if that reward leaves you ill, uninspired and fatigued, you can't help anyone. I learnt this the hard way when I worked for a charity whose mission I deeply resonated with. After 3 years of 70 hour work weeks, I'd lost hair, teeth, direction and, if I'm honest, faith in humanity. It took me 3 years to come back to the light and see that I chose a very stressful job that my body told me repeatedly it could not handle. Travel was a big part of forgiving myself. It helped me put old stories that held me back and probably sent me into this quagmire of self-abuse via work into perspective.

Sometimes we keep letting ourselves make excuses about why we're not travelling because we're scared of the unknown. In such cases, one of three things happens that forces a person from their nest:

- A traumatic event
- Completing a major milestone
- A sudden realisation or epiphany

Do yourself a favour, don't wait for any of those. Decide you want to travel, and book a flight. Our next section takes you through how to book the cheapest possible flight.

HOW TO FIND CHEAP FLIGHTS

"The use of travelling is to regulate imagination by reality, and instead of thinking how things may be, to see them as they are." S amuel Jackson

If you're working full-time you can save yourself a lot of money

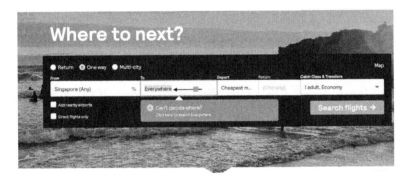

by requesting your time off from work starting in the middle of the week. Tuesdays and Wednesdays are the cheapest days to fly, you can save hundreds just by adjusting your time off.

The simplest secret to booking cheap flights is open parameters. Let's say you want to fly from Chicago to Paris. You need to enter USA to France, you may find flights from NYC to Paris for $70 and can take a cheap flight to NYC. Make sure you calculate full costs, including if you need airport accommodation and of course getting to and from airports, but in every instance open parameters will save you at least half the cost of the flight.

If you're not sure about where you want to go, use open parameters to show you the cheapest destinations from your city.
Use skyscanner.net - they include the low-cost airlines that others like Kayak leave out.

Open parameters can also show you the cheapest dates to fly. If you're flexible you can save up to 80% of the flight cost. Always check the weather at your destination before you book, sometimes a $400 flight will be $20, because its monsoon season. But hey, if you like the rain, why not?

ALWAYS USE A PRIVATE BROWSER TO BOOK FLIGHTS

Skyscanner and other sites track your IP address and put prices up and down based on what they determine your strength of conviction to buy. e.g if you've booked one-way and are looking for the return these sites will jack the prices up by in most cases 50%. Incognito browsing pays.

Use a VPN such as Hola to book your flight from your destination

Install Hola, change your destination to the country you are flying to. The location from which a ticket is booked can affect the price significantly as algorithms take into account local buying power.

Choose the right time to buy your ticket.

Choose the right time to buy your ticket, as purchasing tickets on a Sunday has been proven to be cheaper. If you can only book during the week, try to do it on a Tuesday.

Mistake fares

Email alerts from individual carriers are where you can find the best 'mistake fares". This is where a computer error has resulted in an airline offering the wrong fare. In my experience its best to sign up to individual carriers email lists but if you ARE lazy Secret Flying puts together a daily roster of mistake fares. Visit   to see if there's any errors that can benefit you.

Fly late for cheaper prices.

Red-eye flights, the ones that leave later in the day, are typically cheaper and less crowded, so aim to book that flight if possible. You will also get through the airport much quicker at the end of the day, just make sure there's ground transport available for when you land. You don't want to save $50 on the airfare and spend it on a taxi to your accommodation.

Use this APP for same day flights

If you're plans are flexible, use 'Get The Flight Out' (
) a fare tracker Hopper that shows you
same-day deeply discounted flights. This is best for long-
haul flights with major carriers. You can often find a British
Airways round-trip from JFK Airport to Heathrow for $300. If
you booked this in advance you'd pay at least double.

Take an empty water bottle with you

Airport prices on food and drinks are sky-high. It disgusts
me to see some airports charging $10 for a bottle of water.
ALWAYS take an empty water bottle with you. It's relatively
unknown, but most airports have drinking water fountains
past the security check. Just type in your airport name to
to locate the fountain. Then once
you've passed security (because they don't allow you to
take 100ml or more of liquids) you can freely refill your bottle with water.

Round-the-World (RTW) Tickets

It is always cheaper to book your flights using a DIY approach.
First, you may decide you want to stay longer in one country,
and a RTW will charge you a hefty fee for changing your flight.
Secondly, it all depends on where and when you travel and as
we have discussed, there are many ways to ensure you pay way
less than $1,500 for a year of flights. If you're travelling long-
haul, the best strategy is to buy a return ticket, say New York to
Bangkok and then take cheap flights or transport around Asia
and even to Australia and beyond.

Frequent Flyer Memberships

A frequent-flyer program (FFP) is a loyalty program offered by an airline. They are designed to encourage airline customers to fly more to accumulate points (also called miles, kilometres, or segments) which can be redeemed for air travel or other rewards.

You can sign up with any FFP program for free. There are three major airline alliances in the world: Oneworld, SkyTeam and Star Alliance. I am with One World https://www.oneworld.com/members because the points can be accrued and used for most flights.

The best return on your points is to use them for international business or first class flights with lie-flat seats. You would need 3 times more miles compared to an economy flight, but if you paid cash, you'd pay 5 - 10 times more than the cost of the economy flight, so it really pays to use your points only for upgrades. The worst value for your miles is to buy an economy seat or worse, a gift from the airlines gift-shop.

Sign up for a family/household account to pool miles together. If you share a common address you can claim the miles with most airlines. You can use AwardWallet to keep track of your miles. Remember that they only last for 2 years, so use them before they expire.

Pack like a Pro

"He who would travel happily must travel light." – Antoine de St. Exupery 59.

Travel as lightly as you can. We always need less than we think. You will be very grateful that you have a light pack when changing trains, travelling through the airport, catching a bus, walking to your accommodation, or climbing stairs.

Make a list of what you will wear for 7 days and take only those clothes. You can easily wash your things while you're travelling if you stay in an Airbnb with a washing machine or visit a local laundrette. Roll your clothes for maximum space usage and fewer wrinkles. If you feel really nervous about travelling with such few things make sure you have a dressier outfit, a little black dress for women is always valuable, a shirt for men. Then pack shorts, long pair of pants, loose tops and a hoodie to snuggle in. Remind yourself that a lack of clothing options is an opportunity to find bargain new outfits in thrift stores. You can either sell these on eBay after you've worn them or post them home to yourself. You'll feel less stressed, as you don't have to look after or feel weighed down by excess baggage. Here are three things to remember when packing:

- Co-ordinate colours - make sure everything you bring can be worn together.
- Be happy to do laundry - fresh clothes when you're travelling feels very luxurious.
- Take liquid minis no bigger than 60ml. Liquid is heavy and you simply don't need to carry so much at one time.

Checks to Avoid Fees

Always have 6 months validity on your passport

To enter most countries you need 6 months from the day you land. Factor in different time zones around the world if your passport is on the edge. Airport security will stop you from boarding your flight at the airport if your passport has 5 months and 29 days left.

Google Your Flight Number before you leave for the airport

Easily find out where your plane is from anywhere. Confirm the status of your flight before you leave for the airport with flightaware.com. This can save you long unnecessary wait times.

Check-in online

The founder, Ryan O'Leary of budget airline RyanAir famously said: "We think they should pay €60 for [failing to check-in on-line] being so stupid.". Always check-in online, even for international flights. Cheaper international carriers like Scoot will charge you at the airport to check-in.

Checking Bags

Never, ever check a bag if you possibly can avoid it. It is always cheaper to put heavier items on a ship, rather than take them on a flight with you. Find the best prices for shipping at https://www.parcelmonkey.com/delivery-services/shipping-heavy-items

Use a fragile sticker

Put a 'Fragile' sticker on anything you check to ensure that it's handled better as it goes through security. It'll also be one of the first bags released after the flight, getting you out of the airport quicker.

If you do check your bag, photograph it

Take a photo of your bag before you check it. This will speed up the paperwork if it is damaged or lost.

Relaxing at the airport

The best way to relax at the airport is in a lounge where they provide free food, drinks, comfortable chairs, luxurious amenities (many have showers) and if you're lucky a peaceful ambience. If you're there for a longer time look for Airport Cubicles, sleep pods which charge by the hour.

You can use your FFP Card (Frequent Flyer Memberships) to get into select lounges for free. Check your eligibility before you pay.

If you're travelling a lot I'd recommend to Invest in a Priority Pass for the airport.
It includes 850-plus airport lounges around the world. The cost is $99 for the year and $27 per lounge visit or you can pay $399 for the year all inclusive.

If you need a lounge for a one-off day, you can get a Day Pass. Buy it online for a discount, it always works out cheaper than buying at the airport. Use   .

Lounges are also great if you're travelling with kids, as they're normally free for kids and will definitely cost you less than snacks for your little ones. The rule is that kids should be seen and not heard, so consider this before taking an overly excited child who wants to run around, or you might be asked to leave even after you've paid.

Money: How to make it, spend it and save it while travelling

How to earn money WHILE travelling

"Twenty years from now you will be more disappointed by the things you didn't do than by the ones you did do. So throw off the bowlines. Sail away from the safe harbour." - H. Jackson Brown

Digital nomads receive a lot of hype. Put simply they are "professionals who work online and therefore don't need to tie themselves to one particular office, city, or even country."

The first step in becoming a digital nomad, earning money while travelling is knowing what you can offer. Your market is the whole world. So, what product or service would you like to offer that they would pay for? Take some time to think about this. In German, they say you should do whatever comes easily to your hand. For example, I've always loved finding bargains, it comes very easily for me. Yet I studied Law and Finance at University, which definitely did not come easy. It's no shock that it didn't transpire into a career. And served more as a lesson in not following my ego.

There are thousands of possibilities to generate income while travelling; offering services like tutorial, coaching, writing service pr blogging. Most travellers I meet try their hand at blogging and earning from the advertisements. This is great if you have some savings, but if you need to earn straight away to travel, this should be on the back burner, as it takes time to establish. Still if this comes easily to you, do it!

You want to make good money fast. Ask yourself, what is it that you are good at and how can you deliver maximum value to other people? Here are some ideas if you're totally dumfounded:

1. Teaching English online - you will need a private room for this. Be aware that if you're from the USA and the country you want to work in requires a federal-level background check, it

may take months, so apply early. Opportunities are on: t.vip-kid.com.cn, abc360.com, italki.com, verbalplanet.com and . You can expect to earn $20 an hour.

2. Work in a hostel. Normally you'll get some cash and free accommodation.
3. Fruit picking. I picked Bananas in Tully Australia for $20 an hour. The jobs are menial but can be quite meditative. Look on WWOOF.org for organic farm work.
4. fiverr.com - offer a small service, like making a video template and changing the content for each buyer.
5. Do freelance work online: marketing, finance, writing, App creation, graphic designer, UX or UI designer, SEO optimizer / expert. Create a profile on upwork.com - you need to put in a lot of work to make this successful, but if you have a unique skill like coding, or marketing it can be very lucrative.
6. Make a udemy.com course. Can you offer a course in something people will pay for? e.g. stock trading, knitting or marketing.
7. Use skype to deliver all manner of services: language lessons, therapy, coaching etc. Google for what you could offer. Most specialisms have a platform you can use to find clients and they will take a cut of your earnings/ require a fee.
8. You could work on luxury yachts in the med. Its hard work, but you can save money - DesperateSailors.com
9. Become an Airbnb experience host - but this requires you to know one place and stay there for a time. And you will need a work visa for that country.
10. Work on a cruise ship. This isn't a digital nomad job but it will help you travel and save at the same time.
11. Rent your place out on airbnb while you travel and get a cleaner to manage it. The easiest solution if you own or have a long-term rent contract.

How to spend money

Budget travel hacking begins with a strategy to spend without fees. Your individual strategy depends greatly on the country you legally reside in as to what cards are available. Happily there are some fin-tech solutions which can save you thousands and are widely available globally. I will address those first:

N26
N26 is a 10-year old digital bank. I have been using them for over 6 years. The key advantage is fee-free card transactions abroad. They have a very elegant app, where you can check your timeline for all transactions listed in realtime or manage your in-app security anywhere. The card you receive is a Mastercard so you can use it everywhere. If you lose the card, you don't have to call anyone, just open the app and swipe 'lock card'. It puts your purchases into a graph automatically so you can see what you spend on. You can open an account from abroad entirely online, all you need is your passport and a camera

Revolut
Revolut is a multi-currency account that allows you to hold and exchange 29 currencies and spend fee-free abroad. It's a UK based neobank, but accepts customers from all over the world.

TransferWise debit card
If you're going to be in one place for a long time the The TransferWise debit card is like having your travel money on a card – it lets you spend money at the real exchange rate.

Monzo
Monzo is good if your UK based. They offer a fee-free UK account. Fee-free international money transfers and fee-free spending abroad.

The downside

The cards above are debit cards, meaning you need to have money in those accounts to spend it. This comes with one big downside: safety. Credit card issuers' have "zero liability" meaning you're not liable for unauthorised charges. All of the cards listed above do provide cover for unauthorised charges but times vary greatly in how quickly you'd get your money back if it were stolen.

The best option is to check in your country to see which credit cards are the best for travelling and set up monthly payments to repay the whole amount so you don't pay unnecessary interest. In the USA, Schwab[1] regularly ranks at the top for travel credit cards. Credit cards are always the safer option when abroad simply because you get your money back faster if its stolen and if you're renting cars, most will give you free insurance when you book the car rental using the card, saving you money.

---

[1] Charles Schwab High Yield Checking accounts refund every single ATM fee worldwide, require no minimum balance and have no monthly fee.

Always withdraw money; never exchange.

Money exchanges whether they be on the streets or in the airports will NEVER give you a good exchange rate. Do not bring bundles of cash. Instead withdraw local currency from the ATM as needed and try to use only free ATM's. Many in airports charge you a fee to withdraw cash. Look for bigger ATM's attached to banks to avoid this.

Recap:

- Take cash from local, non-charging ATMs for the best rates.
- Never change at airport exchange desks unless you absolutely have to, then just change just enough to be able get to a bank ATM.
- Bring a spare credit card for emergencies.
- Split cash in various places on your person (pockets, shoes) and in your luggage. Its never sensible to keep your cash or cards all in one place.
- In higher risk areas, use a money belt under your clothes or put $50 in your shoe or bra.

How to save money while travelling

Saving money while travelling sounds like an oxymoron, but it can be done with little to no effort. Einstein is credited as saying, "Compound interest is the eighth wonder of the world." If you saved and invested $100 today, in 20 years it would be $2,000 thanks to the power of compound interest. It makes sense then to save your money, invest and make even more money.

The Acorns app is a simple system for this. It rounds up your credit card purchases and puts the rest into a savings account. So if you pay for a coffee and its $3.01, you'll save 0.99 cents. You won't even notice you're saving by using this app:

Here are some more generic ways you can always save money while travelling:

Device Safety
Having your phone, iPad or laptop stolen is one BIG and annoying way you can lose money traveling. The simple solution is to use apps to track your devices. Some OSes have this feature built-in. Prey will try your smartphones or laptops (preyproject.com).

Book New Airbnb's
When you take a risk on a new Airbnb listing, you save money. Just make sure the hosts profile is at least 3 years old and has reviews.

If you end up in an overcrowded city

The website   is like Airbnb for camping in people's garden and is a great way to save money if you end up in a city during a big event.

Look out for free classes
Lots of hostels offer free classes for guests. If you're planning to stay in a hostel, check out what classes your hostel offers. I have learnt languages, cooking techniques, dance styles, drawing and all manner of things for free by taking advantage of free classes at hostels.

Get a student discount card
If you're studying buy an ISIC card - International Student Identity Card. It is internationally recognised, valid in 133 countries and offers more than 150,000 discounts!

Instal
Maps me is extremely good for travelling without data. It's like offline google maps without the huge download size.

Always buy travel insurance
Don't travel without travel insurance. It is a small cost to pay compared with what could be a huge medical bill.

Travel Apps That'll Make Budget Travel Easier

Travel apps are useful for booking and managing travel logistics. They have one fatal downside, they can track you in the app and keep prices up. If you face this, access the site from an incognito browser tab.

Here are the best apps and what they can do for you:

- Best For flight Fare-Watching: Hopper.
- Best for booking flights: Skyscanner
- Best for timing airport arrivals: FlightAware - check on delays, cancellations and gate changes.
- Best for overcoming a fear of flying: SkyGuru - turbulence forecasts for the route you're flying.
- Best for sharing your location: TripWhistle - text or send your GPS coordinates or location easily.
- Best for splitting expenses among co-travellers: Splittr, Trip Splitter, Venmo or Splitwise.

We have covered the best apps and websites for Adelaide in the section above called useful websites.

How NOT to be ripped off

"One of the great things about travel is that you find out how ma
ny good, kind people there are."
— Edith Wharton

The quote above may seem ill placed in a chapter entitled how not to be ripped off, but I included it to remind you that the vast majority of people do not want to rip you off. In fact, scammers are normally limited to three situations:

1. Around heavily visited attractions - these places are targeted purposively due to sheer footfall. Many criminals believe ripping people off is simply a numbers game.
2. In cities or countries with low-salaries or communist ideologies. If they can't make money in the country, they seek to scam foreigners. If you have travelled to India, Morocco or Cuba you will have observed this phenomenon.
3. When you are stuck and the person helping you knows you have limited options.

Scammers know that most people will avoid confrontation. Don't feel bad about utterly ignoring someone and saying no. Here are six strategies to avoid being ripped off:

1. Never ever agree to pay as much as you want. Always decide on a price before.
Whoever you're dealing with is trained to tell you, they are uninterested in money. This is a trap. If you let people do this they will ask for MUCH MORE money at the end, and because you have used there service, you will feel obliged to pay. This is a con-man's trick and nothing more.

2. Pack light
You can move faster and easier. If you take heavy luggage you will end up taking taxi's which are comparatively very costly over time.

3. NEVER use the airport taxi service. Plan to use public transport before you reach the airport.

4. Don't buy a sim card from the airport. Buy from the local supermarkets it will cost 50% less.

5. Eat at local restaurants serving regional food
Food defines culture. Exploring all delights available to the palate doesn't need to cost huge sums.

6. Ask the locals what something should cost, and try not to pay over that.

7. If you find yourself with limited options. e.g. your taxi dumps you on the side of the road because you refuse to pay more (common in India and parts of South America) don't act desperate and negotiate as if you have other options or you will be extorted.

8. Don't blindly rely on social media

Let's say you post in a Facebook group that you want tips for travelling to The Maldives. A lot of the comments you will receive come from guides, hosts and restaurants doing their own promotion. It's estimated that 50% or more of Facebook's current monthly active users are fake[2]. And what's worse, a recent study found Social media platforms leave 95% of reported fake accounts up[3]. These accounts are the digital versions of the men who hang around the Grand Palace in Bangkok telling tourists its closed, to divert you to

---

2

3

shops where they will receive a commission for bringing you.

It can also be the case that genuine comments come from people who have totally different interests, beliefs and yes, budgets to yours. Make your experience your own and don't believe every comment you read.

Bottom line: use caution when accepting recommendations on social media and always fact-check with your own research.

Small tweaks on the road add up to big differences in your bank balance

Take advantage of other hotel's amenities

If you fancy a swim but you're nowhere near the ocean, try the nearest hotel with a pool. As long as you buy a drink, the hotel staff will likely grant you access.

Fill up your mini bar for free.

Fill up your mini bar for free by storing things from the breakfast bar or grocery shop in your mini bar to give you a greater selection of drinks and food without the hefty price tag.

Save yourself some ironing

Use the steam from the shower to get rid of wrinkles in clothing. If something is creased, leave it trapped with the steam in the bathroom overnight for even better results.

See somewhere else for free

Opt for long stopovers, allowing you to experience another city without spending much money.

Wear your heaviest clothes

on the plane to save weight in your pack, allowing you to bring more with you. Big coats can then be used as pillows to make your flight more comfortable.

Don't get lost while you're away.

Find where you want to go using Google Maps, then type 'OK Maps' into the search bar to store this information for offline viewing.

Use car renting services

Share Now or Car2Go allow you to hire a car for 2 hours for $25 in a lot of Europe.

Share Rides

Use sites like blablacar.com to find others who are driving in your direction. It can be 80% cheaper than normal transport. Just check the drivers reviews.

Use free gym passes

Get a free gym day pass by googling the name of a local gym and free day pass.

When asked by people providing you a service where you are from..

If there's no price list for the service you are asking for, when asked where you are from, Say you are from a lesser-known poorer country. I normally say Macedonia, and if they don't know where it is, add it's a poor country. If you say UK, USA, the majority of Europe bar the well-known poorer countries taxi drivers, tour operators etc will match the price to what they think you pay at home.

Set-up a New Uber/ other car hailing app account for discounts

By googling you can find offers with $50 free for new users in most cities for Uber/ Lyft/ Bolt and alike. Just set up a new gmail.com email account to take advantage.

Where and How to Make Friends

"People don't take trips, trips take people." – John Steinbeck

Become popular at the airport

Want to become popular at the airport? Pack a power bar with multiple outlets and just see how many friends you can make. It's amazing how many people forget their chargers, or who packed them in the luggage that they checked in.

Stay in Hostels

First of all, Hostels don't have to be shared dorms, and they cater to a much wider demographic than is assumed. Hostels are a better environment for meeting people than hotels, and more importantly they tended to open up excursion opportunities that further opened up that opportunity.

Or take up a hobby

If hostels are a definite no-no for you; find an interest. Take up a hobby where you will meet people. I've dived for years and the nature of diving is you're always paired up with a dive buddy. I met a lot of interesting people that way.

When unpleasantries come your way...

We all have our good and bad days travelling, and on a bad day you can feel like just taking a flight home. Here are some ways to overcome common travel problems:

Anxiety when flying

It has been over 40 years since a plane has been brought down by turbulence. Repeat that number to yourself: 40 years! Planes are built to withstand lighting strikes, extreme storms and ultimately can adjust course to get out of their way. Landing and take off are when the most accidents happen, but you have statistically three times the chance of winning a huge jackpot lottery, then you do of dying in a plane crash.

If you feel afraid on the flight focus on your breathing saying the word 'smooth' over and over until the flight is smooth. Always check the airline safety record on airlinerating.com I was surprised to learn Ryanair and Easyjet as much less safe than Wizz Air according to those ratings because they sell similarly priced flights. If there is extreme turbulence, I feel much better knowing I'm in a 7 star safety plane.

Wanting to sleep instead of seeing new places

This is a common problem. Just relax, there's little point do-ing fun things when you feel tired. Factor in jet-lag to your travel plans. When you're rested and alert you'll enjoy your new temporary home much more. Many people hate the first week of a long-trip because of jet-lag and often blame this on their first destination, but its rarely true. Ask travellers who 'hate' a particular place and you will see, that very often they either had jet-lag or an unpleasant journey there.

Going over budget

Come back from a trip to a monster credit card bill? Hopefully this guide has prevented you from returning to an unwanted bill. Of course, there are costs that can creep up and this is a reminder about how to prevent them making their way on to your credit card bill:

-   To and from the airport. Solution: leave adequate time and take the cheapest method - book before.
-   Baggage. Solution: take hand luggage and post things you might need to yourself.
-   Eating out. Solution: go to cheap eats places and suggest those to friends.
-   Parking. Solution: use apps to find free parking
-   Tipping. Solution Leave a modest tip and tell the server you will write them a nice review.
-   Souvenirs. Solution: fridge magnets only.
-   Giving to the poor. (This one still gets me, but if you're giving away $10 a day - it adds up) Solution: volunteer your time instead and recognise that in tourist destinations many beggars are run by organised crime gangs.

Price v Comfort

I love traveling, I don't love struggling. I like decent accommodation, being able to eat properly and see places and enjoy. I am never in the mood for low cost airlines or crappy transfers so here's what I do to save money.

- Avoid organised tours unless you are going to a place where safety is a real issue. They are expensive and constrain your wanderlust to typical things. I only recommend them in Algeria, Iran and Papua New Guinea - where language and gender views pose serious problems all cured by a reputable tour organiser.
- Eat what the locals do.
- Cook in your airbnb/ hostel where restaurants are expensive.
- Shop at local markets.
- Spend time choosing your flight, and check the operator on arilineratings.com
- Mix up hostels and Airbnbs. Hostels for meeting people, Airbnb for relaxing and feeling 'at home'.

Not knowing where free toilets are

Use Toilet Finder - https://play.google.com/store/apps/details?id=com.bto.toilet&hl=en

Your airbnb is awful

Airbnb customer service is notoriously bad. Help yourself out. Try to sort things out with the host, but if you can't, take photos of everything e.g bed, bathroom, mess, doors, contact them within 24 hours. Tell them you had to leave and pay for new accommodation. Ask politely for a full refund including booking fees. With photographic evidence and your new accommodation receipt, they can't refuse.

The airline loses your bag

Go to the Luggage desk before leaving the airport and report the bag missing.
Most airlines will give you an overnight bag, ask where your staying and return the bag to you within three days. Its extremely rare for them to completely lose it due to technological innovation, but if that happens you should submit an insurance claim after the

three days is up, including receipts for everything your had to buy in the interim.

Your travel companion lets you down.

Whether it's a breakup or a friend cancelling, it sucks and can ramp up costs. The easiest solution to finding a new travel companion is to go to a well-reviewed hostel and find someone you want to travel with. You should spend at least three days getting to know this person before you suggest travelling together. Finding someone in person is always better than finding someone online, because you can get a better idea of whether you will have a smooth journey together. Travel can make or break friendships.

Culture shock

I had one of the strongest culture shocks while spending 6 months in Japan. It was overwhelming how much I had to prepare when I went outside of the door (googling words and sentences what to use, where to go, which station and train line to use, what is this food called in Japanese and how does its look etc.). I was so tired constantly but in the end I just let go and went with my extremely bad Japanese. If you feel culture shocked its because your brain is referencing your surroundings to what you know. Stop comparing, have Google translate downloaded and relax.

Your Car rental insurance is crazy expensive

I always use carrentals.com and book with a credit card. Most credit cards will give you free insurance for the car, so you don't need to pay the extra.

You're sick

First off ALWAYS, purchase travel insurance. Including emergency transport up to $500k even to back home, which is usually less than $10 additional. I use https://www.comparethemarket.com/travel-insurance/ to find the best days. If I am sick I normally check into a hotel with room service and ride it out.

Make a Medication Travel Kit

Take travel sized medications with you:

- Antidiarrheal medication (for example, bismuth subsalicylate, loperamide)
- Medicine for pain or fever (such as acetaminophen, aspirin, or ibuprofen)
- Throat Lozenges

Save yourself from most travel related hassles

- Do not make jokes with immigration and customs staff. A misunderstanding can lead to HUGE fines.

- Book the most direct flight you can find, nonstop if possible.

- Carry a US$50 bill for emergency cash. I have entered a country and all ATM and credit card systems were down. US$ can be exchanged nearly anywhere in the world and is useful in extreme situations, but where possible don't exchange, as you will lose money.

- Check, and recheck, required visas and such BEFORE the day of your trip. Some countries, for instance, require a ticket out of the country in order to enter. Others, like the

US and Australia, require electronic authorisation in advance.

- Airport security is asinine and inconsistent around the world. Keep this in mind when connecting flights. Always leave at least 2 hours for international connections or international to domestic. In London Stansted for example, they force you to buy one of their plastic bags, and remove your liquids from your own plastic bag…. just to make money from you. And this adds to the time it will take to get through security so lines are long.

- Wiki travel is perfect to use for a lay of the land.

- Expensive luggage rarely lasts longer than cheap luggage, in my experience. Fancy leather bags are toast with air travel.
-

Food

- When it comes to food, eat in local restaurants, not tourist-geared joints. Any place with the menu in three or more languages is going to be overpriced.
- Take a spork - a knife, spoon and fork all in one.

Water Bottle

Take a water bottle with a filter. We love these ones from Water to Go.
Empty it before airport security and separate the bottle and filter as some airport people will try and claim it has liquids…

Bug Sprays

If you're heading somewhere tropical spray your clothes with Permethrin before you travel. It lasts 40 washes and saves space in your bag. A 'Bite Away' zapper can be used after the bite to totally erase it. It cuts down on the itching and erases the bite from your skin.

Order free mini's

Don't buy those expensive travel sized toiletries, order travel sized freebies online. This gives you the opportunity to try brands you've never used before, and who knows, you might even find your new favourite soap.

Take a waterproof bag

If you're travelling alone you can swim without worrying about your phone, wallet and passport laying on the beach. You can also use it as a source of entertainment on those ultra budget flights.

Make a private entertainment centre anywhere

Always take an eye-mask, earplugs, a scarf and a kindle reader - so you can sleep and entertain yourself anywhere!

The best Travel Gadgets

The door alarm

If you're nervous and staying in private rooms or airbnbs take a door alarm. For those times when you just don't feel safe, it can help you fall asleep. You can get tiny ones for less than $10 from Amazon:

Smart Blanket

Amazon sells a 6 in 1 heating blanket that is very useful for cold plane or bus trips. Its great if you have poor circulation as it becomes a detachable Foot Warmer: Amazon http://amzn.to/2hTYlOP I paid $49.00.

The coat that becomes a tent

https://www.adiff.com/products/tent-jacket. This is great if you're going to be doing a lot of camping.

Clever Tank Top with Secret Pockets

Keep your valuables safe in this top. Perfect for all climates.

on Amazon for $39.90

Optical Camera Lens for Smartphones and Tablets
Leave your bulky camera at home. Turn your device into a high-performance camera. Buy on Amazon for $9.95

Travel-sized Wireless Router with USB Media Storage

Convert any wired network to a wireless network. Buy on Amazon for $17.99

Buy a Scrubba Bag to wash your clothes on the go
Or a cheaper imitable. You can wash your clothes on the go.

Hacks for Families

Rent an Airbnb apartment so you can cook

Apartments are much better for families, as you have all the amenities you'd have at home. They are normally cheaper per person too. We are the first travel guide publisher to include Airbnb's in our recommendations if you think any of these need updating you can email me
at philgtang@gmail.com

Shop at local markets

Eat seasonal products and local products. Get closer to the local market and observe the prices and the offer. What you can find more easily, will be the cheapest

Take Free Tours

Download free podcast tours of the destination you are visiting. The podcast will tell you where to start, where to go, and what to look for. Often you can find multiple podcast tours of the same place. Listen to all of them if you like, each one will tell you a little something new.

Pack Extra Ear Phones

If you go on a museum tour, they often have audio guides. Instead of having to rent one for each person, take some extra earphones. Most audio tour devices have a place to plug in a second set.

Buy Souvenirs Ahead of Time

If you are buying souvenirs someone touristy, you are paying a premium price. By ordering the same exact products online, you can save a lot of money.

Use Cheap Transportation

Do as the locals do, including weekly passes.

Carry Reusable Water Bottles

Spending money on water and other beverages can quickly add up. Instead of paying for drinks, take some refillable water bottles.

Combine Attractions

Many major cities offer ticket bundles where one price gets you into 5 or 6 popular attractions. You will need to plan ahead of time to decide what things you plan to do on vacation and see if they are selling these activities together.

Pack Snacks

Granola bars, apples, baby carrots, bananas, cheese crackers, juice boxes, pretzels, fruit snacks, apple sauce, grapes, and veggie chips.

Stick to Carry-On Bags

Do not pay to check a large bag. Even a small child can pull a carry-on.

Visit free art galleries and museums

Just google the name + free days.

Eat Street Food

There's a lot of unnecessary fear around this. You can watch the food prepared. Go for the stands that have a steady queue.

Travel Gadgets for Families

Dropcam

Are what-if scenarios playing out in your head? Then you need Dropcam.

'Dropcam HD Internet Wi-Fi Video Monitoring Cameras help you watch what you love from anywhere. In less than a minute, you'll have it setup and securely streaming video to you over your home Wi-Fi. Watch what you love while away with Dropcam HD.'

Approximate Price: $139

Kelty-Child-Carrier

Voted as one of the best hiking essentials if you're traveling with kids and can carry a child up to 18kg.

Jetkids Bedbox

No more giving up your own personal space on the plane with this suitcase that becomes a bed.

Safety

"If you think adventure is dangerous, try routine. It's lethal." – Paulo Coelho

Backpacker murdered is a media headline that leads people to think traveling is more dangerous than it is. The media sensationalise the rare murders and deaths of backpackers and travellers. The actual chances of you dying abroad are extremely extremely low.

Let's take the USA as an example. In 2018, 724 Americans **died** from unnatural causes, 167 died from car accidents, while the majority of the other deaths resulted from drownings, suicides, and non-vehicular accidents. Contrast this with the 15,000 murders in the US in 2018, and travelling abroad looks much safer than staying at home.

There are many thing you can to keep yourself save. Here are out tips.

1. Always check fco.co.uk before travelling. NEVER RELY on websites or books. Things are changing constantly and the FCO's (UK's foreign office) advice is always UP TO DATE (hourly) and extremely conservative.
2. Check your mindset. I've travelled alone to over 180 countries and the main thing I learnt is if you walk around scared, or anticipating you're going to be pickpocketed, your constant fear will attract bad energy. Murders or attacks on travellers are the mainstay of media, not reality, especially in countries familiar with travellers. The only place I had cause to genuinely fear for my life was Papa New Guinea - where nothing actually happened to me only my own panic over culture shock.

There are many things you can do to stop yourself being victim to the two main problems when travelling: theft or being scammed.

I will address theft first. Here are my top tips:

- Stay alert while you're out and always have an exit strategy.
- Keep your money in a few different places on your person and your passport somewhere it can't be grabbed.
- Take a photo of your passport on your phone incase. If you do lose it, google for your embassy, you can usually get a temporary pretty fast.
- Google safety tips for traveling in your country to help yourself out and memorise the emergency number.
- At hostels keep your large bag in the room far under the bed/ out of the way with a lock on the zipper.
- On buses/trains I would even lock my bag to the luggage rack.
- Get a personal keychain alarm. The sound will scare anyone away.
- Don't wear any jewellery. A man attempted to rob a friend of her engagement ring in Bogota, Colombia, and in hindsight I wished I'd told her to leave it at home/wear it on a hidden necklace, as the chaos it created was avoidable.
- Don't turn your back to traffic while you use your phone.
- When traveling in the tuktuk sit in the middle and keep your bag secure. Wear sunglasses as dust can easily get in your eyes.
- Don't let anyone give you flowers, bracelets, or any type of trinket, even if they insist it's for free and compliment you like crazy.
- Don't let strangers know that you are alone - unless they are travel friends ;-)
- Lastly, and most importantly -Trust your gut! If it doesn't feel right, it isn't.

Hilarious Travel Stories

I have compiled these short stories from fellow travellers to pick you up when you're feeling down. Life on the road isn't always easy and we've all had those days when we want to stay in bed and forget the world exists. Laughter is the best way I know to shake those feelings. All people who have shared these stories wanted to remain anonymous. After reading them I think you'll understand why…

I mentioned my wife earlier, so its only fair she be the first story. Don't worry she has given me permission to share.

A marriage up the wall

'Delhi belly got me on the third day into the trip to India. I was vomiting so much that I couldn't keep even water down so I went to a health clinic for tourists. Whilst I was there I was asked to poop into a jar and happily put on a drip.

The doctor attending me was mid to late 40's and very creepy. I decided I'd leave the clinic after my 4th bag of fluids because I felt better and was weirded out by the intense stares of my doctor. As I was paying the bill, the doctor came over, dropped to one knee and asked me to marry him at the desk. I stuttered in shock that I was already was married. He was holding a jar of my poo in his hand, stood and then chucked it at the wall. The jar broke open and my watery specimen was literally smeared across the wall as he trudged off. The woman serving me bobbed her head from side to side as if we were discussing the weather and said 'its not personal madam, you look like his last wife.'

Glass shame

'I was in Nashville airport in the smoking room. I heard my name being called for my flight so I rushed out but instead of rushing through the door, I walked smack into the glass. When I opened the door the entire departure lounge was roaring with laughter.'

The Dashing Date

'I had a date with a fellow Brit in Medellin. I went to the bathroom and when I came back, I asked him if he had paid the bill and he replied 'yes'. We were going down some stairs when he suddenly shouted at me to run. Yes, the restaurant staff were running after us because he hadn't paid.'

A fear of farting in hostels

'When I arrived to stay in my first ever hostel in London, I realised I had an intense fear
farting in my sleep. I literally gave myself such bad constipation I had to go to hospital. It turns out an enema is worse than hostel farting.'

What a boob
I fell on the Tube in London getting into a carriage. Unfortunately I managed to grab a woman's boob on the way to the floor. I was so mortified I walked everywhere else during the trip.'

Cementing a few laughs

'I was walking on the streets in Singapore when they were fixing the roads. I somehow stepped in fresh cement. I only noticed when my feet became so heavy I thought I had twisted my ankle. The cement got so hard, I had to take them off as I couldn't pick up my feet. Locals were very clearly entertained as I walked in my sponge bob squarepants socks.

If you've got a hilarious travel story you'd love to share, email me at   . All identifying details will be removed.

How I got hooked on budget travelling

'We're on holiday' is what my dad used to say to justify getting us in so much debt we lost our home and all our things when I was 11. We moved from the suburban bliss of Hemel Hempstead to a run down council estate in inner-city London, near my dad's new job as a refuge collector, a fancy word for dustbin man. I lost all my school friends while watching my dad go through a nervous breakdown.

My dad loved walking up a hotel lobby desk without a care in the world. So much so, that he booked overpriced holidays on credit cards. A lot of holidays. As it turned out we couldn't afford any of them. In the end, my dad had no choice but to declare bankruptcy. When my mum realised he'd racked up so much debt our family unit dissolved. A neat and perhaps as painless a summary of events that lead me to my life's passion: budget travel that doesn't compromise on fun, safety or comfort.

I started travelling full-time at the age of 18. I wrote the first Super Cheap Insider guide for friends visiting Norway - which I did for a month on less than $250. When sales reached 10,000 I decided to form the Super Cheap Insider Guides company. As I know from first-hand experience debt can be a noose around our necks, and saying 'oh come on, we're on vacation' isn't a get out of jail free card.

Before I embarked upon writing Super Cheap Insider guides many, many people told me that my dream was impossible, travelling on a budget could never be comfortable. I hope this guide has proved to you what I have known for a long-time: budget travel can feel luxurious when you know and use the insider hacks.

And apologies, if I depressed you with my tale of woe. My dad is now happily remarried and works as a chef in London at a fancy hotel - the kind he used to take us too!

A final word...

There's a simple system you can use to think about budget travel. In life we can choose two of the following: cheap, fast or quality. So if you want it Cheap and fast you will get a lower quality service. Fast-food is the perfect example. The system holds true for purchasing anything while travelling. I always choose cheap and quality, except in times where I am really limited on time. Normally you can make small tweaks to make this work for you. Ultimately you must make choices about what's most important to you.

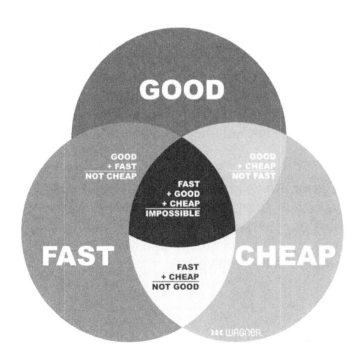

Our Writers

Phil Tang was born in London to immigrants, Phil graduated from The London School of Economics with a degree in Law. Now he travels full-time in search of travel bargains with his wife, dog and 1 year old daughter.

Ali Blythe has been writing about amazing places for 17 years. He loves travel and especially tiny budgets equalling big adventures nearly as much as his family. He recently trekked the Satopanth Glacier trekking through those ways from where no one else would trek. Ali is an adventurer by nature and bargainist by religion.

Michele Whitter writes about languages and travel. What separates her from other travel writers is her will to explain complex topics in a no-nonsense, straightforward way. She doesn't promise the world. But always delivers step-by-step methods you can immediately implement to travel on a budget.

Kim Mortimer, Kim's input on Super Cheap Insider Guides show you how to stretch your money further so you can travel cheaper, smarter, and with more wanderlust. She loves going over land on horses and helps us refine each guide to keep them effective.

Copyright

Published in Great Britain in 2019 by Super Cheap Insider Guides LTD.

If you've found this book useful, please consider leaving a short review on Amazon it would mean a lot.

Our Mission   6

Redefining Super Cheap   12

Discover Adelaide   14

Planning your trip   17

Hack your Adelaide Accommodation   20

The best price performance location in Adelaide 26

Use our FREE   27

accommodation finder service   27

How to be a green tourist in Adelaide   29

Saving money on Adelaide Food   31

SNAPSHOT: How to enjoy a $1,000 trip to Adelaide for $200   33

Unique bargains I love in Adelaide   34

Exchange Rate   35

How to use this book   36

OUR SUPER CHEAP TIPS…   37

Getting around   37

Start with this free tour   38

Go to a Free museum   40

Do a wine tour on the cheap   41

Visit the University   42

Cycle to Waterfall Gully   43

Visit the Adelaide Oval   44

Explore 29 parks   45

Henley Beach   46

Explore Adelaide Central Market   47

Visit Glenelg Beach   48

Explore Hahndorf   49

The Murray River   50

Enjoy free workouts   51

Get Cheap cinema tickets   52

Cheap Tuesday at the fringe festival   52

Food and drinks hacks   53

Nightlife   54

Not super cheap but loved   55

Visit Port Hughes   56

Swim with sea lions   57

Visit Kangaroo Island   58

Walk the Heysen Trail   59

Explore the outback   60

Cheapest route from the USA   63

Cheapest route from Europe   64

Need to Know   65

Cheap Eats   66

Avoid these tourist traps or scams   68

Religion   68

FREQUENTLY ASKED QUESTIONS 69

Getting out cheaply 70

Print or screenshot for easy reference 72

RECAP: How to have a $1,000 trip to Adelaide on a $205 budget 73

Ultimate Cheat Sheet 75

Thank you for reading 81

Bonus Budget Travel Hacks 85

How to find the freedom to travel 87

HOW TO FIND CHEAP FLIGHTS 91

Frequent Flyer Memberships 95

Pack like a Pro 96

Checks to Avoid Fees 97

Relaxing at the airport 99

Money: How to make it, spend it and save it while travelling 101

How to earn money WHILE travelling 102

How to spend money 104

How to save money while travelling 107

Travel Apps That'll Make Budget Travel Easier 109

How NOT to be ripped off 110

Small tweaks on the road add up to big differences in your bank balance 113

Where and How to Make Friends 116

When unpleasantries come your way…   117

Your Car rental insurance is crazy expensive   120

The best Travel Gadgets   125

Hacks for Families   127

Safety   130

Hilarious Travel Stories   132

How I got hooked on budget travelling   135

A final word…   137

Our Writers   138

Copyright   139

HOW DID WE DO?

1 DID WE SAVE YOU MONEY?

2 DID YOU LEARN INSIDER INSIGHTS?

3 DID YOU GET A LIST OF THE BEST CHEAP EATS?

4 DID WE HELP YOU PLAN TO SAVE AND ENJOY MORE?

WHAT CAN WE DO BETTER?

EMAIL ME: PHILGTANG@GMAIL.COM

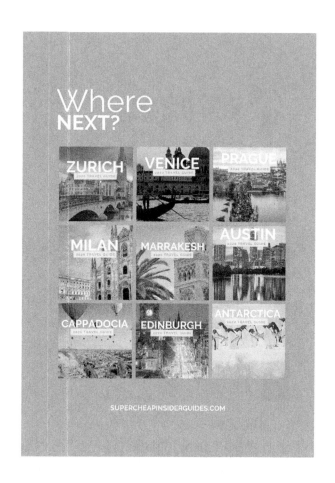